Charles F. Deems

The Gospel of Common Sense as Contained in the Canonical Epistle

of James

Charles F. Deems

The Gospel of Common Sense as Contained in the Canonical Epistle of James

ISBN/EAN: 9783337285920

Printed in Europe, USA, Canada, Australia, Japan

Cover: Foto ©Lupo / pixelio.de

More available books at **www.hansebooks.com**

THE
GOSPEL OF COMMON SENSE

AS CONTAINED IN THE

CANONICAL EPISTLE OF JAMES

BY

CHARLES F. DEEMS, D.D., LL.D.
PASTOR OF THE CHURCH OF THE STRANGERS

NEW YORK
WILBUR B. KETCHAM
13 COOPER UNION
EDINBURGH, SCOTLAND: JAMES GEMMELL

Copyright, 1888, by Charles F. Deems.

TO THE

REV. DR. GUSTAV GOTTHEIL,

RABBI OF THE TEMPLE EMMANU-EL, NEW YORK,

AND TO

RT. REV. HENRY C. POTTER,

BISHOP OF THE DIOCESE OF NEW YORK,

WHO PRESENT EXCELLENT TYPES,

ONE OF WHAT JAMES WAS AS AN ISRAELITE

AND THE OTHER WHAT HE WAS AS A CHRISTIAN

THIS BOOK IS DEDICATED,

WITH PERMISSION, BY THEIR FRIEND AND BROTHER,

ITS AUTHOR.

PREFACE.

Life is practical. Men need plain rules for their daily guidance. Plain rules depend on principles. Principles are abstract, and belong to the domain of philosophy. We owe incalculable debts to the men who work in this department; but they are cut off from the sympathy of the mass of mankind, who cannot appreciate their labors.

There is, however, something which can be appreciated by us all, namely, the plain teaching of those rules by which daily life is guided. It is a good sign that there is an increase of books on ethics, books which can be understood by even those who are so unlearned as not to know what the word "ethics" means.

This volume is in that line. The Hebrew and Christian Sacred Scriptures are not only authoritative in religion; they are rich in ethics. A visible life constructed on the Decalogue, the Book of Proverbs, the Sermon on the Mount and the Epistle of JAMES would fill the loftiest, broadest and most beautiful outline of manhood. The Epistle of JAMES has always been a great favorite with the writer of these pages. He never sympathized with the estimate once placed upon it by Luther, who called it an "epistle of straw," because it was not robust with theological discussions like the Pauline writings. This estimate Luther lived long enough and grew wise enough to change. That great scholar and teacher, the late Roswell D. Hitchcock, LL.D., with whose friendship I was honored, once said that the application of the Epistle of JAMES in the region of economy is that which alone can save our civilization, and it is reported of the third Earl of Balcarras that he was accustomed to express himself as delighted with the Epistle of JAMES as "the production of a gentleman."

It seems fitting that the teaching of this admirable Letter should be so expounded as to be adapted to men's surroundings in this day. To that task the author has addressed himself.

While everything has been excluded from his pages which could be suspected of indicating a desire to appear learned, the author feels sure that all real scholars will perceive that he has not written without research. For business-men, workingmen, busy women, young people and simple souls more than for the learned, this volume has been written in the earnest hope that its perusal will quicken the conscience and shape the life of the reader. No Greek in the New Testament seems so beautiful as that of the writer of the Epistle of JAMES; it has been a pleasure to make a new and careful translation thereof for the author's own use: this he has interwoven with the discussion of the text for the benefit of those who know nothing of Greek.

This is not a volume of sermons. Ordinarily that which is fit to be preached is unfit to be printed. The rhetoric of appeal to the jury is not the style of address to the court. But all the discussions in this

Preface. vii.

volume were loosened out and inflamed for the pulpit and delivered in a series of discourses in the Church of the Strangers, in New York, in the spring of 1888. They were listened to by thousands of hearers from different parts of the country, among whom were some Israelites and some Hebrew-Christians, and to the frequent request, by letter or otherwise, from those who heard is chiefly due the determination to publish this volume.

It will be perceived that this book is dedicated to a Jewish Rabbi and a Christian Bishop. Both men have been long known and highly regarded, and each has shown me valued personal kindnesses. Each gave me permission to make the dedication; but I think it due to both to state that neither knew anything of any views set forth in any portion of the book, and neither is at all responsible for anything it contains: and I think I ought to add, each was too considerate to hedge himself by even requesting the making of this statement. Each knows that I am a Protestant Christian, and believes that, while I fearlessly announce my convictions, I am incapable of wantonly assailing anything loved and revered by any sect of devout Christians or Israelites.

CHURCH OF THE STRANGERS,
 NEW YORK.

CONTENTS.

I.

INTRODUCTORY TO THE EPISTLE OF JAMES, pp. 13-27.
Authorship.—Catholic Epistles.—Epistle of James.—The Women at the Cross.—Perpetual Virginity.—The Mary and Her Sons.—The Lord's Brother.—Some Account of James.—Characteristics of James.—Date and Motive of Epistle.—Present Use of Epistle.

II.

INTRODUCTORY MATTER OF THE EPISTLE, pp. 28-66.
Salutation.—A Great Man's Modesty.—The Greeting.—Trials of Life: A Wrong Theory.—Special Sources of Trouble.—Joy in Trials.—What is Temptation?—Grounds of Rejoicing.—God's Providence.—Effect of Trial.—"Perfect" and "Entire."—The Giving God.—What is Wisdom?—Every True Prayer Answered.—Doubts.—Specific Forms of Trouble.—From Low to High.—From High to Low.—A Higher Thought.—The Faithless Poor cannot Rejoice.—The Faithless Rich cannot Rejoice.—The Faithful Rich.—Happiness in Trials.

III.

TEMPTATION TO VISIONARINESS, pp. 67-86.
Unworthy Thoughts of God.—Origin of Evil.—Not in God.—In the Individual.—Heredity.—Environment.—The Genesis of Evil.—"Drawn Away" and "Enticed."—Companions and Amusements.—Plan of the Seducer.—A Horrible Picture.—A Great Error.—A Great Truth.—The Father of Lights.—The Changeless Father.

IV.

THE NEW LIFE VERSUS FANATICISM, pp. 87–109.

Regeneration.—Fanaticism.—Swift to Hear and Slow to Speak.—Slow to Wrath.—Preparation of Heart.—Listening to Preaching. The Ingrafted Word.—The Law of Liberty.—A Mistake as to Religion.—Religion in Character.—A Life of Beneficence.—A Life of Purity.

V.

THE TEMPTATION TO PARTIALITY, pp. 110–132.

Partiality for the Rich.—Going to Court.—Evil of Partiality.—On the Side of the Poor.—On the Side of the Rich.—A Reply to the Partialist.—A Great Principle.—A Necessary Principle.—A Guarded Expression.—Choose Mercy.

VI.

FAITH AND WORKS, pp. 133–150.

Justification.—Paul and James.—Theology and Ethics.—The Practical Test.—Facts of Experience.—The Case of Abraham.—The Philotheans.—The Case of Rahab.—Frederick W. Robertson's Illustration.—Archbishop Whately's Illustration.

VII.

TEMPTATIONS OF THE TONGUE, pp. 151–187.

Fanaticism and the Tongue.—The Tongue in Public.—The Tongue in Private.—The Great Responsibility.—Danger of the Tongue.—The Mental Tubercle.—A Perfect Man.—Tongue and Pen.—A Publisher's Responsibility.—Satan's Tongue.—One Untamable Thing.—Religious Uses of the Tongue.—Source of the Evil.—"Wisdom" and "Knowledge."—Two Wisdoms.—Wisdom from Above.—Characteristics.—A Cheering Promise.

VIII.

DEMONIACAL WISDOM, pp. 188-198.

Fruits Thereof.—False Christs.—Evils of War.—Whence come Wars.—The Fruitlessness of Sin.—Prayer.

IX.

WORLDLY-MINDEDNESS, pp. 199-233.

Reproaches.—The Religious Covenant a Marriage.—The Love of God and Worldly-mindedness.—"Lover of the World."—Holy Scripture against Worldly-mindedness.—The Holy Spirit against Worldly-mindedness.—God is against Pride.—True Conversion.—Submission to God.—No Morality Possible to Atheism.—Who is a Moral Man?—What is a Devil?—Why Men do not Submit to God.—Drawing Nigh to God.—Case of Abraham.—Case of Moses.—Case of Isaiah.—Cleansed Hands.—Evil Speaking.—Contradiction.—Evil Hearing.—The Mosaic Law.—One Lawgiver.—The Restless Spirit.—Self-confidence.—"Deo Volente."

X.

THE SINFULNESS OF USELESSNESS, pp. 234-254.

A Principle of Varied Application.—Sins of "Omission" and "Commission."—Process of Descent.—Process of Ascent.—The Acted Parable.—The Destructive Napkin.—Sin in Purple.—The Last Judgment.—The Nearest First.—The Implication of Altruism.—Knowledge Aggravates Sin.—The Money Illustration.—Four Ways Open.

XI.

IMPENDING JUDGMENT, pp. 255-270.

XII.

The Final Theme, pp. 271-322.

Patience.—Time a Factor.—The Sin of Grumbling.—Example of the Prophets.—Illustrious Gentile Sufferer.—Against Oaths.—Vows in Trouble.—Temperance Pledges.—Conjuration.—Profanity.—Its Utter Uselessness.—Judicial Oaths.—Prayer Cure.—The Early Congregational Order.—Charismata.—Sickness and Sin.—Visiting the Sick.—Confession.—The Last Sentence.—Truth.—Error.—Creed.—A Grand Possibility.—Covering Sin.—True Liberty.—Immortal Fame.

THE GOSPEL OF COMMON SENSE.

I.

Introductory to the Epistle of James.

THE CATHOLIC EPISTLES.

IN the arrangement of the earliest collection of Christian literature, the Evangely has the precedence. Then follows "The Acts of the Apostles," containing the beginnings of the history of Christianity. That wonderful series of letters, written by the Apostle Paul to several of the earliest churches, contained such a body of philosophical, ethical, and religious teaching as naturally to form a most important section in itself. Then there existed the writings of other Apostles, having equal authority with the writings of Paul, namely, the Epistle of James, the two Epistles of Peter, the three Epistles of John, and the Epistle of Jude. To these seven was given the title "The Catholic Epistles."

They were so called probably because they were not addressed to particular churches, but to the Church at large. Even the second and third of

John, although they have a personal address, are so constructed as to be edifying to the whole body of Christians everywhere.

THE EPISTLE OF JAMES.

The authorship of the first of the Catholic Epistles probably all students have found, with Neander, to be the most difficult question in Apostolic history. The difficulty possibly arises from the commonness of the name James, or Jacobus, among the Jews at the time of Jesus, and the slightness of the specific notice of some who bear the name. Let us see if we can make it out.

When our Lord was crucified there were four women who were witnesses of the awful scene, Mary, the mother of Jesus, and her sister Salome, who was wife of Zebedee; Mary, the wife of Clopas, sometimes called Alphæus, and Mary Magdalene. The last was unmarried; the third was probably the sister of Joseph, and so sister-in-law of the mother of Jesus, or Joseph's brother may have been Clopas. The second was the Mother-Mary's own sister. Each of the married women seems to have had a son named James. Salome Zebedee was the mother of James, the brother of John; Mary Clopas was the mother of James the Less; and our Lord's mother had among the sons and daughters born to her after Jesus a son named James.

Let us read over the record to make this clear to us. John 19: 25, reads "There were standing by the cross of Jesus His mother, and His mother's sister, Mary [the wife] of Clopas, and Mary Magdalene." In Matthew 27 : 56, three women are mentioned, "Mary Magdalene and Mary the mother of James [the Less] and of Joses, *and* the mother of Zebedee's children." In Mark 15 : 40, the record is in this order: "Mary Magdalene, and Mary the mother of James the Less and of Joses, and Salome." Luke gives no catalogue.

RELATIONS OF THE WOMEN AT THE CROSS.

Several interesting things are to be seen in these passages. They settle the fact that there were four distinguished women at the cross. They show that our Lord's mother's sister, His aunt, named Salome, had married Zebedee and become the mother of James and John, so that John was first cousin to Jesus, not on the side of His putative father, Joseph, but on the side of His real mother, Mary. It is to be remarked that in Matthew and Mark the name of Mary of Magdala heads the list. She seems to have been the dearest person on earth to Jesus. Perhaps John was next. A very lovable men was he. Like all very lovable men he had his little human weaknesses. With all his excellent qualities, the record represents him as irascible, vain and ambitious. Was he also a little jealous? He puts Mary Magdalene last, while the others put her first. He places his mother next to the mother of the Lord as he would have placed himself and his brother, the one on the right and the other on the left of the Lord, when He should come in His glory (Matt. 20: 21). Moreover, the indirectness of his manner in speaking of himself as the disciple, "whom Jesus loved" (John 13:23), comes out in his designation of his own mother as Jesus's mother's sister.

Now, two of these women had each a son called James, namely Salome Zebedee and Mary Clopas. Was either of these the author of the epistle? It certainly was not James Zebedee, who was beheaded A.D. 44 or, as some suppose, A.D. 41. He was the first of the Apostles who gained martyrdom (Acts 12:2). James the Less is mentioned as an Apostle by each of the Evangelists and in the Acts of the Apostles. But there is still a third James mentioned. In the Epistle to the Galatians, Paul records a visit which he made to Peter at Jerusalem. This occurred when Paul had been converted at least three years. He says (1:19): "But other of the Apostles saw I none, save James the Lord's brother." "The Lord's brother," who is he? Between him and the little James does not the authorship of the epistle rest?

PERPETUAL VIRGINITY.

For centuries the run of comment on the family relations of Jesus was in favor of considering James the Less, the son of Alphæus (who was supposed to be the same as Clopas), as one of those called the "brothers" of the Lord. Great ingenuity has been expended on this theory, but nothing could sustain it a moment in the presence of common sense if there had not been some hypothesis to be sustained. That hypothesis was *the perpetual virginity of Mary, the mother of Jesus*. To the assumption of that as a fact was to be reconciled the existence of such facts and passages as the following :

THE MARY AND HER SONS.

Mary and her "sons" are associated in frequent mention. While He yet talked to the people, behold "His mother and His brethren stood without" (Matt. 12 : 46). This phraseology shows that the relation of these parties to Jesus must have been generally known. In the next verse it is recorded, "Then one said to Him : 'Thy mother and Thy brethren stand without, desiring to speak to Thee.'" In Mark 3:31, a similar phrase is used : "There came then His brethren and His mother," and in Luke 8 : 19, the very same phrase. At the beginning of His public ministry (John 2 : 12) "He went down to Capernaum, He and His mother, and His brethren, and His disciples." All this represents a family, a family keeping close together. What have the boys of Clopas and his wife Mary to do with this family ?

We find that James, the son of Clopas, believed in Jesus, and was actually one of the Apostles at a time when the brothers of Jesus did not believe on Him (John 7 : 5), among whom must have been His brother JAMES. The same man could not be at once an apostle and an infidel.

In the first chapter of the Acts of the Apostles there is a simple and touching description of the state of affairs after the ascension of Jesus into heaven. From the Mount of Olives the Apostles returned to Jerusalem and established a sort of Christian community. The list of the eleven Apostles is given in detail, and amongst them is the name of "James, the son of Alphæus," or Clopas. Then it is added, "These all continued with one accord in prayer and supplication with the women, and Mary, the mother of Jesus, and *with His brethren.*" Plainly James, the son of Alphæus, was not of "His brethren."

THE LORD'S BROTHER.

Returning to the passage in Galatians (1 : 19), we must recollect that Paul knew the names of the Apostles and their relations to one another. He went to Jerusalem to pay a visit to Peter, "to become acquainted with Peter" are his words. He must have known that "James, the son of Alphæus," or Clopas, was an Apostle. But he says that he saw "not one other Apostle"; then he did not see James the Less; but he says that he *did* see another distinguished Christian whom he calls "James, the Lord's brother."

In face of this record resort must be had to the very contradictory theory that somehow or other the *James* of Alphæus was so a member of the family of Mary as to be called her "son" and the "brother" of Jesus. If in the Epistle to the Galatians, Paul had written "Thomas," or "Bartholomew," or "Philip," or any other name, the same ingenuity would have been expended and with the same result. The foolish doctrine of the perpetual virginity of Mary was to be maintained. It was founded on the belief that in man celibacy is a virtue, and that in woman virginity is a state of sanctity, and is superior to motherhood. This bad doctrine has done much to pervert the ideals and corrupt the morals of Christendom. The opposite must be taught. Men and women must learn that celibacy when it is of a man's choice, or a woman's, is a crime against God, against nature and society, and that the man or woman who passes through life without achieving parentage has been living in sin, unless it can be shown that there is physical disability or other plainly marked providential hindrance. This pernicious doctrine brought weakness to Christianity in the earlier centuries, did much to fill the middle ages with a large and bad crowd of unmarried women and men, and is in the latter part of the nineteenth century doing a vast harm in circles of married as well as of unmarried people. Every pastor in a great city who has the intimate confidence of the people must have learned that much ruin has come to the bodily, mental and spiritual health of both men and women by habits produced by the belief that motherhood was a thing to be avoided or, at least, that virginity was preferable to motherhood. The very moment Mary began in any sense to be the mother of Jesus, she ceased to be a virgin. It was no one other than the Holy Ghost which supplanted her virginity with motherhood: and once a mother, she would naturally, as a good young woman, if she lived decently with her husband, become a mother again.

The most natural is the easiest theory in this case. It requires no ingenious twisting of the record and no strained explanation of any passage in the Holy Scripture. Mary had at least seven children, *Jesus*, the miraculously begotten who is called her "*first*-born son" (Luke 2:7), four other sons, one of whom was named James, and at least two daughters, all the children of Joseph by Mary, and begotten in lawful wedlock. This is the natural reading of Matt. 13:55, 56. It had been a hard providence to make Joseph perpetually childless in return for his devoutly beautiful behavior under the trying circumstances of Mary's condition during their espousal.

The name of James is given as that of the author of this epistle. It is most reasonable to believe that it must have been one of the three Jameses intimately associated with the career of our Lord. It has been shown that it could have been neither John Zebedee's brother James nor James Clopas, called James the Less. As Mary, the mother of Jesus, had four sons, the eldest of whom was named James and called "the brother of the Lord," all historical and moral probabilities point to him as the author of the epistle.

SOME ACCOUNT OF JAMES.

JAMES, "the brother of the Lord" (Gal. 1 : 19), became a convert to Christianity after the resurrection of our Lord. He was held in high repute by the Jews and by the Apostles. According to Eusebius (Eccles. Hist. 2 : 1), he was the first pastor (overseer or bishop) of the Church at Jerusalem, and was surnamed *The Just* on account of his eminent virtues. The Apostles all looked up to him. When Peter was brought out of the prison to the house of Rhoda (Acts 12) he sent a special announcement thereof to JAMES. In the council held at Jerusalem, probably A.D. 53, to settle the controversy between Paul and Barnabas on the one side, and certain Judaizing teachers who insisted that the Gentile converts should be circumcised, after all had spoken it was JAMES who gave the decision.

The importance of this council and of the influence of JAMES will justify giving space to the following extract from Milman's "History of Christianity" (I., 403):

"The barrier was now thrown down, but Judaism rallied, as it were, for a last effort behind its ruins. It was now manifest that Christianity would no longer endure the rigid nationalism of the Jew, who demanded that every proselyte to his faith should be enrolled as a member of his race. Circumcision could no longer be maintained as the seal of conversion, but still the total abrogation of the Mosaic law, the extinction of all their privileges of descent, the substitution of a purely religious for a national community, to the Christianized Jew, appeared, as it were, a kind of treason against the religious majesty of their ancestors. A conference became necessary between the leaders of the Christian community to avert an inevitable collision which might be fatal to the progress of the religion. Already the peace of the flourishing community at Antioch had been disturbed by some of the more zealous converts from Jerusalem, who still asserted the indispensable necessity of circumcision. Paul and Barnabas proceeded as delegates from the community at Antioch; and what is called the Council of Jerusalem, a full assembly of all the Apostles then present in the metropolis, solemnly debated this great question. How far the earlier Apostles were themselves emancipated from the inveterate Judaism does not distinctly appear; but the situation of affairs required the most nicely balanced judgment united with the utmost moderation of temper. On one side, a Pharisaic party had brought into Christianity a rigorous and passionate attachment to the Mosaic institutes in their strictest and most minute provisions. On the other hand, beyond the borders of Palestine, far the greater number of converts had been formed from that intermediate class which stood between Heathenism and Judaism. There might seem, then, no alternative but to estrange one party by the abrogation of the Law, or the other by the strict enforcement of all its provisions. Each party might appeal to the divine sanction. To the eternal, the irrepealable sanctity of the Law, the God of their fathers, according to Jewish opinion, was solemnly pledged; while the vision of Peter, which authorized the admission of the Gentiles into Christianity, still more the success of Paul and Barnabas in proselyting the heathen, accompanied by undeniable manifestations of divine favor, seemed irresistible evidence of the divine sanction to the abrogation of the Law, as far as concerned the Gentile proselytes. The influence of JAMES effected a discreet and temperate compromise: Judaism, as it were, capitulated on honorable terms."

CHARACTERISTICS OF JAMES.

This remarkable deliverance reveals two of the striking characteristics of JAMES, namely, his strong adherence to the old form of the faith in Judaism, and his rare common sense, by which he saved the new form of the faith from unnecessary collision with Judaism. A decision which pleased "the Apostles" (even Paul and Peter as well as the others), "and elders with the whole Church," must have been founded on a common sense of a very high order. It was a blessed thing for the first church in Jerusalem and for early Christianity among the Gentiles and for our Holy Faith ever since, that the first pastor in Jerusalem was not Paul, nor Peter, nor John, but the wiser, more prudent, more discreet JAMES, the brother of the Lord. These two characteristics of an ardent Jewish sentiment and surpassing common sense appear in his epistle, which is the first in order of the Catholic Epistles, and is addressed "to the twelve tribes scattered abroad." That it was addressed to those Christians who had been Jews rather than Gentile Christians shows where his heart lay. The pastor of the church in Jerusalem could not lose sight of the sheep of his flock even when they were scattered through Judea and Samaria (Acts 8:1) and perhaps still further abroad. They were endeared to him by the national relationship, and bound to him by the bond of the Faith, "the faith of our Lord Jesus Christ, the Lord of glory" (2:1); and he was "a servant of God, even of the Lord Jesus Christ" (1:1), and was sustained by the hope of "the coming of the Lord" (5:7), with which he sought to fortify his suffering brethren who had fled before the storm of persecution then raging in the Holy City.

The pastoral office in his day was not so much one of authority as of influence. If it had been the former, Paul or Peter would have filled it. It appears to have been reached by personal influence, of which JAMES seems to have had much more than any of the other brethren, and on that account was more influential and more useful, being more free from dogma and more pervaded with the spirit of persuasiveness.

THE DATE AND MOTIVE OF THE EPISTLE.

The date of the writing of the epistle is uncertain and unimportant for our purposes. From the allusion to the fact that his readers bore the name of "Christians" (2:7), the letter was probably written after that name was given in Antioch to the followers of our Lord (Acts 11:26). But it must have been some years after that event, and indeed even after the Council at Jerusalem, A.D. 53 (Acts 15), as the presupposition of a wide knowledge of Christian doctrines and terms indicates.

It was evidently not the intention of JAMES to address to his Hebrew-Christian brethren a letter on Christian doctrine. He was not discussing the nature of saving faith, but he was discussing and denouncing an unsaving faith, a reliance of many of his brethren on the fact that they were the children of Abraham, which made them feel that that was sufficient for salvation without those good works which are always the product of saving faith. It seems absurd to suppose that JAMES wrote to counteract the teaching of Paul. A critical examination of JAMES'S epistle does not reveal a single fact which suggests that the writer had in his mind any thought of anything that had proceeded from the pen of Paul. Indeed, there is no evidence that he had seen any of Paul's epistles, and very probably wrote his own before Paul's Epistle to the Romans was written (which was not until A. D. 60), certainly before it had gained any circulation among the early Christian churches, in which epistle Paul elaborately sets forth his doctrine of justification by faith. Indeed it would seem to be the object of JAMES to bring his readers to such a living faith as is set forth by his brother Paul, "a faith that *worketh* by love" (Gal. 5 : 6).

The epistle is plainly meant to inculcate morals. The writer does not seek to reach this end by setting forth a systematic ethical treatise, but rather by warning his readers against such sins and errors as they would naturally fall into because of their early Jewish and late Christian circumstances, and to exhort them to such a course of holy living as would justify them to themselves in showing that they really had such faith in the Lord Jesus Christ as made them fruitful as well as unblamable. It was an effort to lift them off their sandy position and place them on a foundation of rock. Indeed in this epistle one is constantly reminded of the Sermon on the Mount, and the Apostle seems to have been a very close student of that wonderful discussion on *Character* delivered by his brother Jesus. These two sons of Mary were much alike in some mental characteristics, and the so-called Sermon on the Mount delivered to Jews and the Epistle of JAMES delivered to Christians will ever remain the most valuable text-books on morals in possession of the world.

THE PRESENT USE OF THE EPISTLE.

Are they so broad, so catholic, so ecumenical, so free from the swaddling clothes of the world's infancy, so suited to man as man that nineteenth-century folk can have benefit from the study of them? We believe that they are, and that the Epistle of JAMES especially, more than anything else in the New Testament, seems as if it might have been privately written A.D. 1888 for New York and London, for California and Germany; as if the writer had taken a tour of inspection among the synagogues and churches of our day, and written in kindly expostulation and exhortation, to turn his Jewish and Christian brethren away from their errors, and confirm them in a large, strong life of fidelity, and chastity, and charity.

In that belief, and as much as possible in the spirit of JAMES, we make a study of his epistle, and shall endeavor to draw from it the lesson needed by us amid the cares and perplexity, the engrossments, the pleasures and the pressures of the present age.

II.

Introductory Matter of the Epistle.

CHAPTER I., 1–12.

THE SALUTATION TO HEBREW-CHRISTIANS.

THE salutation bears the characteristics of JAMES. It is terse, full, and rhetorical. *"James, of God and of the Lord Jesus Christ the bond-servant, to the twelve tribes which are in the dispersion, hail."* The collocation of the words shows a recognition of the faith under the two forms of Judaism and Christianity. All that was divine in Judaism, JAMES still held as not being at all weakened by his faith in Jesus; and his devotion to Jesus did not affect in the slightest degree his devotion to the God of his fathers. Indeed, he seems to suggest the thought that no conscientious Jew who, in the spirit of his father Abraham, follows out the teachings of Moses and the prophets can fail to become finally a servant of God by being a servant of that *Jesus* whom God has *christened*, anointed to be *Lord*, the ruler of the world. On the other hand no man can be a servant of that Jesus who is the Christ Lord without receiving all that is moral and religious in the monotheism set forth in the writings of Moses and the prophets as the sure basis of any growing spiritual life. A Christian receives everything which gives divine instruction and comfort to his Jewish brother. What had been necessary to spiritual culture in the earlier day, but had discharged its function, he does not hold binding as any part of the ritual or spirituality of true religion, but every intelligent and right-hearted Christian reveres those stars which shone before the sun arose. Having the antitype he has no need to depend wholly on the type ; having the fulfilment he has no need to live entirely on the prophecy for his spiritual growth, but he reverently studies the type and preserves the prophecy, seeing that the constant comparison of the fulfilment with the prediction is a constant strengthening of his faith.

It would really in our day seem to be a question whether any man who knows the Gospel can be a full and faithful servant of the God of Abraham, and of Isaac, and of Jacob, who is not at the same time a faithful and devoted servant of Jesus, God's anointed Ruler. On the other hand, how can a man be a full and faithful servant of Jesus, the Christ Lord, who is not devoted to the service of the God of the children of Israel, that God who anointed Jesus to be the world's Lord ? If the Israelitish religion be considered defective without that in the Christian faith for preparation of which the elder faith existed ; so, utterly emptied, not only of all power but of all life, would be the Christian religion if deprived of any of the spiritual elements which vitalized that religion which lifted Moses to the heights of God, and wrapt Isaiah in the flames of inspiration, and kindled in David the fires which melted in him the truth that has run molten and singing down the centuries. The ideal which we should all seek to attain is that which is expressed in the twin-name of *Hebrew-Christian.* Such was JAMES.

A GREAT MAN'S MODESTY.

See the modesty of this great man. He had received the first thrill of his life in the womb which had held Him whom the world was to receive as the Son of God. He had played with the holy child Jesus in the house of Joseph and Mary, and down in the Nazareth streets close by the Fount of the Virgin. He had grown up under the spell of the matchless character of the wonderful brother whose life was made sublime and simple by the great work which He had to do. With Him JAMES had climbed the heights above Nazareth, and descended the slopes into the plain below, and in long, deep, earnest talks had received into himself, under the eye of their pure and exalted mother, a formative element which told powerfully upon his own character. He had watched this elder brother's growth in stature and wisdom and grace, until the time He entered upon a ministry begun by the miracle at Cana of Galilee, at which JAMES probably was present. He had endured all the intellectual perplexity which arose from knowing that Jesus was his brother just as the other sons of Mary were, so far as he could perceive, and yet had always had some exaltation, some spiritual element which made Him so divinely far apart while He was so humanly near. JAMES was probably married, and was not living with the Mother-Mary when Jesus was crucified. He had never given in his allegiance to Jesus as the Messiah, as the Lord of Humanity, as the Savior of the world until that crucified Brother had been buried, had raised Himself from the dead, had shown Himself to Peter, then to the Twelve and then to five hundred disciples, and then to this brother, who had not believed on Him. This overwhelming interview had thoroughly converted JAMES, and prepared him to be the pastor of the first Christian church in Jerusalem and the helper of all Christian people in all time to come. So he humbly calls himself, "the bond-servant of God and of the Lord Jesus Christ."

The title "bond-servant" or "slave" distinguishes the bearer from that of "hireling." It meant one who was "bound," not a mere wage-taker, but bound for life, so bound that his interests and his master's had become inseparably united, so that he could not be faithless to his master without injury to himself, and that the master's interest lay in taking care of the bond-servant.

"Now, from the *devotedness* of such service," says Bishop Bloomfield (on Romans 1 : 1), "it was applied to the service of God, and the term *servant of God* was applied first to Moses and Joshua, afterwards to the Apostles and the ministers of the Gospel in general, as in 2 Tim. 2 : 24, in both which last uses, it denotes one devoted to the spiritual service of Christ in His Gospel; and, therefore, indicates both the *station* and the *devotedness* of the person to whom it is applied." Yet if JAMES did have any thought of "station," he certainly suggests it modestly. He makes no great claim of authority as coming from his station. He relies more upon the influence coming from his character. He claims nothing as "the brother of the Lord," although he was commonly known in Christian circles by that appellation.

THE GREETING.

The "greeting" is to be noticed. It comes at the beginning of the epistle as it does in the circular letter which JAMES sent to the churches at the close of the Council at Jerusalem, and it is in the same abbreviated form (Acts 15 : 23). Strictly translated the word means "to be happy." "I tell (you) to be happy" would be the full phrase.

It occurs negatively in 2 John 10 : "If any one cometh unto you and bringeth not this teaching, receive him not into your house, and do not tell him to be happy."

The address is made to his Hebrew-Christian brethren of every part of the nationality, and so he calls them the "twelve tribes." The frequent scatterings of the Jews seem to have wrought an obliteration of the tribal distinction, so that now it may be said that for about twenty centuries they have been without that distinction and without king or government, without temple and priest. But when the ten tribes were carried away some individuals had remained and some had returned. When Josiah undertook to purge Judah and Jerusalem, B.C. 628, they were still in the land, and recognized by their tribal relations, as it appears that the good young king carried his reformation to "the cities of Manasseh, and Ephraim, and Simeon, even unto Naphtali" (2 Chron. 34 : 1–6). In the ninth verse of the same chapter, we learn that contributions were made to the temple-fund by Manasseh, Ephraim and "all the remnant of Israel." In the Book of Ezra (6 : 21) mention is made of the children of Israel who had come again out of their captivity, and that at the dedication of the House of God there were offered "for a sin-offering for *all Israel, twelve he-goats*, according to the number of the tribes of Israel." That these persons for themselves took an interested part in the joyful solemnities appears from the statement (Ezra 8 : 35) that "the children of those that had been carried away, which were come out of the captivity, offered burnt offerings to the God of Israel, twelve bullocks for all Israel," etc. This was B.C. 457. But everywhere there were descendants of the original families of all the tribes, and Paul sympathized with the religious patriotism of JAMES, as appears in the phrase occurring in his plea for himself before Agrippa, in which he speaks of " our twelve tribes, instantly serving God day and night " (Acts 26: 7).

THE TRIALS OF LIFE: A WRONG THEORY.

The writer lost no time with ceremonious preliminaries. The object for which he had undertaken the epistle was always before him. He knew that those to whom it was addressed were having a doubly hard life; hard because they were Jews, and hard because they were Christians.

Life is not always easy to any, of whatever condition or fortune. And men increase the painfulness of living by undertaking life on a wrong theory: namely, the conception of the possibility of making life free from trouble. They dream of this; they plan for this; they toil for this; they are all disappointed. It is impracticable. After millions of failures in all the past, and the sight of failure in all lives visible to us, each man renews the efforts to accomplish the impossible. He might just as well seek to live without eating or without breathing. In the present condition of human society, no man is born to be free from trouble. On the contrary, all human beings are born to trouble as the birds fly upward. (This seems to be the meaning of Job 5, 7.)

The metaphor of the birds is instructive. It is of a bird's nature to fly. The build of its body, with its adjusted apparatus, suggests flying. The law of heredity has transmitted to each bird the natural impulsion to fly. Resting is the interruption of a bird's flying, not the contrary. Flying is his rule; walking or resting, his exception. The fish was made *to* swim, as the bird was made *to* fly, and man was "born *to* trouble." There are intervals. In the life of each of us, as we have passed out of a great trouble, it has seemed as if no more would come. But another has come; and our lives are spent in being in some trouble, or in passing from one trouble to another.

If there be any exception to that rule — if there be any man or woman on the planet past thirty, who has had no troubles, I have never seen that person or heard that person's name. Have you?

Why, then, should we increase the difficulties of human life by adding to its natural limitations the attempt to reach the unattainable? They live the less difficult lives who early adjust themselves to the natural fact that trouble is to be the normal condition of life. They prepare themselves for it. They fortify themselves by philosophy and religion to endure the inevitable. Then every hour free from trouble is so much clear gain. But to him who adopts the other theory—and who does not?—every trouble is so much clear loss. The man in trouble, the fish in water, the bird in air: that is the law; why not accept it?

That fact need not discourage us. It does not take from our dignity, nor from our growth, nor from our final happiness. The painter cannot have his picture glowing on the canvas by merely designing it, nor the sculptor transmute his ideal into marble by a wish. The one must take all the trouble of drawing and coloring, and the other that of chiselling and polishing. It is no necessary discouragement to a boy that he must be under tutors, and must go through the trouble and discipline of school days, even if he be a prince. *It is the law.* That answers all. It need scarcely be added that for any success we must conform to the law. Our whole human experience has taught that lesson. I am not responsible for the law. I did not make it. I cannot alter it; most certainly I would not abrogate it, unless I be a born and unchangeable fool. There are only two courses left. I can obey the law, and thus adjust myself to my physical and spiritual environment, or I can resist the law, and thus do for myself what the earthen pitcher would do for itself if it dashed itself against the stone curb of the well.

This sure view of life is not pessimistic. It detracts nothing from the theory of the harmony of the universe, any more than the shades of color or the parts of music detract, the former from the harmony of the picture, or the latter from the harmony of the tune. It is a very untrue estimate of life to regard it as successful in proportion to the absence of trouble.

SPECIAL SOURCES OF TROUBLE.

The men to whom JAMES wrote this epistle had several sources of trouble. They were exiled from their birth-place, or the birth-place of their fathers; they were exiled from their church-home; their Christian profession naturally excluded them from the sympathies of their former co-religionists; their own natural attachment to their old forms of worship and methods of expressing their earnest beliefs distinguished them so from their new Gentile fellow-Christians that they did not find perfect sympathy there; and, as Jews, they were exposed to all the depressions which came to them from their Roman conquerors on account of their nationality, and as Christians, to all the suppressions attempted by the same civil power on account of their religion. These they had in addition to the troubles which naturally fell to them as men.

The good JAMES saw all this. There was nothing vague and dreamy in him. He took direct and clear views of life. He knew how their condition of suffering would have a tendency to depress his scattered brethren. He would strengthen that he might cheer them. He knew that any other method of dealing would be of no permanent value to them. The very opening of his address is a vigorous tonic; and his whole epistle, written in the most beautiful Greek found in the New Testament, is of an epigrammatic style of thought uttered in sparkling language.

What was good for them must be good for us, so far as it goes to form character by stimulating our ethical qualities. In these pages it is proposed to give a study to this epistle, not a critical examination, not a specially philosophical analysis, but a plain, common-sense inquiry into the meaning of the teaching of the most practical of all the early propagators of the teaching of Jesus.

JOY IN TRIALS.

Immediately after his salutation, the writer breaks upon his readers almost as with a shout, "*My brethren, count it all joy when ye fall into divers temptations.*" He puts himself into sympathetic communication with them at once. "*My brethren*," he calls them; as though he would remind them that what he was about to say was not a lecture delivered by a stranger, by a cold professor of ethical science, but a heart-talk by a brother in tribulation who, in his own experience, had acquired ample knowledge of the kind of sorrow which often burdened their hearts.

He strikes a high key in the beginning. "All joy!" Why, most of them seemed to have almost no joy. "Divers trials" they had: that was a condensed statement of their normal circumstances. Now he prefers to show them that those divers trials, coming upon them from different quarters, attacking them on different sides, could rationally be counted by them as "all joy."

WHAT IS TEMPTATION?

It is to be observed that "temptations" as the word is rendered in the Common Version does not mean seduction to evil. In the 13th verse of the first chapter, JAMES writes: "Let no man say when he is tempted, *I am tempted of God;*' for God cannot be tempted of evil, neither tempteth He any man." And JAMES knew that his brother Jesus had taught a prayer to His disciples, a prayer oftener repeated perhaps than any other form of address to God in any language, a prayer in which we are to ask the Father in heaven to "lead us not into temptation," that is, providentially to bring to bear upon us such influences as shall lead us away from seduction to evil.

"When ye fall into divers trials!" The word here must mean just what it means in the twelfth verse of this chapter: "Blessed is the man that endureth *temptation*, for when he *is tried*, he shall receive the crown of life."

Very carefully does the writer, by his choice of language, guard against any mistake. He exhorts no man, Jew or Gentile, Christian or infidel or reprobate, to rejoice in trouble brought upon himself by his sins or his imprudences. In the very constitution of things, the man that has done wrong must suffer; when the punishment comes he has little ground for rejoicing, but much for abasement and sorrow; and well is it for that man if his sorrow worketh in him repentance. So Paul wrote to the Corinthians (2 Cor. 7 : 9): "Now I rejoice not that ye were made sorry, but that ye were made sorry unto repentance."

In this world trouble will come to all. The very processes of nature by which we and our children are brought into the world and carried out of the world, the necessary results of our affections, which give such charm and glow to life, all bring us unavoidable trouble. Probably the most of our troubles, and greatest, come through our affections. Adam and Eve loved Cain and Abel. When one of the brothers slew the other, the bereaved parents had double trouble. They had lost a child. In proportion to the goodness of that son, his obedience and filial love, was the poignancy of the anguish of bereavement. That was a great trouble. It was the first death of a human being. But there was a greater trouble. The loss of the slain lay not so heavy on the hearts of the first parents as the guilt of the slayer. On one side was a loss, on the other a crime. They had a son who was dead and another who was a murderer.

Who can estimate the trouble brought upon husbands by the wrong-doing of their wives, upon wives by their husbands, upon parents by their children, and upon children by their parents? If all the sorrow which comes upon men by the wrong-doing of others could instantly be removed from the world, how immensely the trouble of the race would be mitigated. The world would seem to resemble heaven. Indeed, the Sacred Scriptures represent the escape from the world as an entrance upon the state where "the wicked cease from troubling."

When these troubles are upon men they may be made seductions to evil or trials of character. The work of the evil spirit is to render them temptations in the bad sense. Our Heavenly Father uses them as trials. The men who have no faith in the God of Abraham, the God and Father of Jesus Christ, have no right to rejoice either when they bring temptations upon themselves by their vices or fall into temptations in the ordinary process of affairs. There is a "sorrow of the world" which "worketh death" (2 Cor. 7:10). But Abraham and JAMES, and all others who are Israelites, and true Christians, and most especially those who, like the persons to whom this epistle was addressed, were Christian

Israelites, have great reason to count it "all joy" when they "fall into divers" troubles, which the Heavenly Father makes "divers [or versi-colored] trials" and so manifold blessings. So true is it that while the grace of God, like a celestial alchemy, extracts only good from evil, the malignity of Satan, like an infernal magic, draws evil out of good.

GROUNDS OF REJOICING.

Why should Christians rejoice when they "fall into divers temptations"?

GOD'S PROVIDENCE.

Because it comes in the providence of God, for which the servants of God have no responsibility. They have not ordered the affairs of the universe, and they have not violated that order. There is no fault on either side. There could not be a world so good as this, and be a world in which there were no trouble. That has been settled by the believer once for all. He cannot join the cry of the rebellious heart when it asks, in passionate anger, "Why does God take *my* beloved to the grave? Why does God allow this trouble to come upon me?" He does not ask for a constant interference upon the part of God, with the operations which He has set at work in a universe conceived in infinite love, and produced in infinite wisdom, and sustained by the incessant exercise of infinite power. There has been no caprice in the Immortal Father, and no sin in the mortal child. Walking on the path of duty, the Father's child has fallen into trouble. He counts it all joy that he did not make the trouble, and that his Father knew that it found him on the path of duty. The servant of our Lord Jesus, the child of Abraham, should take as a governing principle of his life, the sentiment that a grain of guilt is heavier than ten tons of trouble.

A devout and intelligent soul knows that God his Father is not an unconcerned observer of the movements of the universe. Having fashioned that orderly universe, He governs it on certain principles; but He has never surrendered the government of that universe, or turned it loose, to go of itself. While certain effects come from certain causes, even feeble men can control those effects, and combine them and use them as causes for other effects. Much more can God. His general providence is seen in the operation of the laws He has set for the government of things. A part of those laws may be scientifically ascertained by His children who have "pleasure in His works." But who knows them all? If there be some laws of matter and of mind which it is impossible for human beings to discover, will not God reveal those also? Will He not, in all conditions and circumstances, use what He Himself has produced, so as to carry forward in the best way the highest education of His child? The true son and servant of the Lord believes that his Heavenly Father adapts His special providence to the particular case of each of His children. He may not interfere to stop the operation of the laws He has wisely ordained; but He will bring other laws to operate upon the results so as to benefit His children. He may not keep the fire from burning a heroic saint who rushes in to pluck a sinner from the flaming house; but He will bring to that saint from his torturing wound and ugly scar a glory princes cannot gain from crowns.

THE EFFECT OF TRIAL.

There is great comfort and often much joy in reflecting upon the effect of all the discipline of trouble if rightly used. It is the development of that in man which not only distinguishes him from the lower animals, but is that which is the loftiest and most ennobling of human capabilities, namely *faith*. To be able to perceive, to compare, to judge, to reason, to remember, to fancy, to imagine, these are wonderful intellectual endowments. But a much greater faculty than any one of them and than they all, is that faculty which enables us to receive and to cling to the truth; and that is faith. What were all others without this? Of what use would my senses be if I could not have faith in the correctness of their report? Of what use my logical understanding if I could have no faith in conclusions produced by its processes? Without faith it is plainly impossible to have any physical science or any science of the mind. Without faith it is impossible to have any system or any practical life. No wonder then that it has been said that without faith " it is impossible to please God," seeing that without faith it is impossible to please either our fellow-men or ourselves.

Then, what a man most needs is the certainty that his faith is genuine. This can be ascertained only by some such process as that which an assayer employs when he strives to discover the ingredients of any substance. The testing of gold ore, for instance, is a process involving several mixtures, several vessels, and several uses of great heat. It is important to know what proportion of gold there is in the ore. There may be other things in combination; but the assayer is intent on finding how much of the ore is gold. The ore is more valuable as there is more gold in it. There may be silver, there may be lead, there may be copper, and these are useful metals; but it is the *gold* which gives the chief value to the ore. So it is faith which gives chief value to any man. Great imagination may make a great poet; great logical powers, a great philosopher; great faculty for observation, a great scientist; but *nothing makes a great man but great faith.*

Now afflictions are trials of one's faith. JAMES uses the word which signifies a " test," and a test applied in such a way as to produce proof of the correctness of the result. The argument of the author is : "*Since ye know—which we take for granted—that afflictions are trials,* [tests] *of faith, and since ye also know that it is this testing of your faith which produces endurance*" (v. 3). The test takes other things away and leaves the faith ; not only that, but it leaves also the proof that it is genuine faith.

"PERFECT" AND "ENTIRE."

This endurance, which the writer seems to consider the finally desirable thing, may have two meanings : it may signify the being able to bear whatever is laid on us by our Lord, and which we call *patience*, or it may signify *permanence of character*. The latter seems the fixed meaning. Before the blast the dead leaves are driven, or the waves on the surface of the ocean are tossed, but the tree has endurance and remains ; the ocean has endurance and remains. It is this *permanence* of character which is desirable above all things. The earlier trials are the first weights imposed upon character. They tend to give compactness. There is a line of density below which no substance can be pressed. Every additional pound of weight causes that which is pressed to approach that compactness which no additional burden can increase.

This completed compactness the writer calls the "perfect work" of endurance. The sooner a man reaches this effect of trouble, the sooner is he at the point where no trouble can ever work him any harm. He is "perfect and entire."

The words "perfect" and "entire" are not synonymous. There is a difference quite worth noticing: the first being properly applied to what has reached its end—that which has reached its complete development—in the case of a tree, to that which is full grown; the second, to that which has all that belongs to it—in the case of an heir, to one who has obtained the last item of the estate to which he is entitled. Through this whole letter we are to recollect that it was first addressed to Hebrew-Christians.

The writer of this epistle did not understand Judaism and Christianity as two religions. He had come to believe that Judaism was not perfected until it developed into Christianity; that was the intention of Judaism, which had been a tree in process of development, and not complete until it bore the flowers and fruits of Christianity. The Israelite who had developed into a Christian was "perfect." While he remained only a Jew, he was heir to a vast estate, upon a large and rich portion of which he had not entered until he became a Christian; then he was "entire."

To us perhaps the most practical distinction in the meaning of the words may point to a difference in faith and practice, in the inner spiritual life and outer active life. The result of all trials should be to increase that perfect faith which works by love and makes the life entire.

When the writer adds "lacking nothing," "*in nothing left behind*," pointing by the word he employs to a race, perhaps he would intimate to us, that there might be danger of misinterpreting what he had written so as to signify that where a Hebrew had developed into a Christian there was nothing more to do. He knew that however far the racers had run, the race was not won while there remained any space uncovered. The discipline should prepare us to make further progress. The Christian individual and the Christian Church must each grow in grace and in the knowledge of our Lord and Savior. The result of all past discipline from pain, is to prepare us to trust more, to learn more, to love more. To stop runing is to lose the race; to stop growing is to begin to decay.

THE GIVING GOD.

The writer seems to hear some of his readers say: "But it requires much wisdom to live thus in the midst of trials." Very true! But the supply is at hand. "*Ask of God.*" "*If any of you come short of wisdom let him ask of the giving God.*" What an encouraging epithet, "the giving God,"—the God who is accustomed to give, who is known amongst men and angels as THE GIVER. And that there may be the utmost encouragement, JAMES gives three characteristics of His giving: (1) It is universal, (2) it is abundant,* and (3) it is unselfish. How exceedingly encouraging this is.

One may say, "I am so insignificant;" another, "I am so sinful;" another, "I have so little faith;" another, "I am so hard."

But you are a human being, and He gives to *all*.

"But I am so fearfully lacking, my need of wisdom is so great. If I had any sense whatever, I might apply to Him." But, He "giveth liberally." He longs to have great things asked of Him. Go to little men for little things. It is as easy for a great man to do a great thing, as for a small man to do a small thing. God, the Father, King of the world, may be asked for the largest gifts, since no giving can possibly render Him poorer. John Newton has this thought in one of his hymns:

> "Thou art coming to a King,
> Large petitions with thee bring:
> For His grace and power are such
> None can ever ask too much."

A humane monarch once said, "The greatest advantage of being a king is, that the king has the power to make so many happy." The advantage which God has over all His children—even earthly monarchs—is that He has more power to make more people happy.

---

¹ Acts 17: 25, "He giveth to all life and breath and all things."

The unselfishness of the Divine Giver is seen in that He never "upbraids." Human givers are so interested in their part of any giving transaction that a much-solicited person is apt to do or say something which shall remind the receiver of his obligation, and to make former gifts a reason for withholding that which is now sought ; and, more especially, if good use has not been made of former benefactions, to upbraid the ungrateful or thriftless receiver. Even human parents sometimes do this. It requires the greatest nobility to rise above such inclinations. Our Father never upbraids. He never points to the misuse we have made of any former gifts. He never tires of giving, and so He never says to a penitent at His feet : "What, you here again ! Can you never be satisfied ? Where is the blessing I gave you last week ? There seems to be no hour of the day or night in which you are not soliciting something." No ! He never says such things. He is so delighted to have us ask that He would have us more ashamed of not coming to Him for needed wisdom than for any other fault or sin.

WHAT IS WISDOM ?

The wisdom we are to seek may be that wisdom which will enable us to turn every trouble to a good account. He is a great merchant who can make a great commercial disaster the foundation of a fortune. He is a great general who can wrench victory from defeat. He is a wise man who grows stronger in the midst of troubles which break weaker men.

Or, it may be that exalted nobility of spirit which JAMES describes (3 : 17) as produced by the wisdom which cometh down from above.

Or, it may be that same religiousness which is named in Holy Scripture as "the fear of the Lord," which fear the Psalmist (111 : 10) calls "the beginning of wisdom," and (112 : 1) describes as great delight in the commandments of the Lord. Still earlier, in the Book of Job (18 : 28) it had been written: "Behold, the fear of the Lord, that is wisdom; and to depart from evil is understanding."

EVERY TRUE PRAYER ANSWERED.

How positive is the assurance of an answer to this prayer for wisdom! You may pray for a change of circumstances, for more land or money, or for success in some undertaking, or for deliverance from some trouble; and the Father may see that it is better to leave you just as you are, and answer your prayer in some other way. In some way for good every true prayer is answered. There could not possibly be an unanswered prayer without something greater than a miracle—without a revolution of the whole system of the universe. Until attraction repels, and heat makes cool, and effects produce their own causes, there cannot be an unanswered prayer, because God has ordained the connection between the real prayer, intellectually meant and heartily felt prayer, with the production of some spiritual good. The law of gravity is not more sure in its existence, or more unerring in its action, than the law of spiritual prayer. But, as in physical, so in spiritual operations, the result does not always come in the anticipated mode, but it comes somehow. The law of equivalents is unfailing. But there is one prayer which we *know* the Father will answer. There is no "perchance" here. We need not say, "If it please Thee," as we do when we are praying for the recovery of some beloved person who is sick. It may be better that the sick should die. It was expedient that Jesus should depart. So, while His disciples prayed and hoped that He might stay, He went. But their prayers for His remaining were answered with a blessing greater than the continuing of His bodily presence with them could have been. There are no conditions in asking God for wisdom. "He that seeks" it "*shall* find." The petitioner may present his prayer as a claim, and demand the answer of this special prayer as the fulfilment of God's special promise.

All the more may he do so, because this wisdom is something no man can have by inheritance, and no man acquire by any study under the best teachers and amidst the best circumstances, and no man can impart to his fellow-man. For this wisdom we must "ask of *God*."

But the prayer for it must be in faith. The soul of the petitioner must be in the attitude of certain expectancy. The heart must be lifted up with the eyes. This can be done with perfect simplicity if the prayer be for that which God has surely promised. The petitioner can then go from his house knowing that it has been done, just as certainly as he can know in any other way that anything else has been done; just as the telegraph operator knows that his message has gone, after he has touched the keys. There is no question further; there are no contingencies. When he does not know what God's will is, he says, "If it be Thy will." But he does not say that when God has stated in advance what His will is.

DOUBTS NEUTRALIZE.

Of course no blessing comes if the man doubts. God could not give in such a case, because the man could not receive. When the Father has promised His wisdom, a special spiritual gift, how can it rule me if I close all the avenues of my spirit by my unbelief? The object of the gift is to improve the relations between the Father and the child, but manifestly that cannot begin to be done if the child believes that the Father is a liar, or even if he fail to have the most perfect faith in the honor and good intentions of the Father. He must not doubt. If he is not willing to give God *trust*, how can he expect God to give him *wisdom?*

For a doubting man is like a sea-surface. He is superficial. He lies open to all disturbing influences, as the ocean does on its surface, on which every wind plays, driving it forward and piling it into waves. Such is what JAMES calls a double-souled man. There are few greater misfortunes than to be thus between two natures. Instability destroys the value of all that is good in a man. "Unstable as water, thou shalt not excel," said the patriarch Jacob to one of his sons.

A two-souled man is unsettled; *"unstable in all ways."* His opinions are fluctuating; and so are his sentiments. Sometimes he is repenting of his sins, and sometimes he is repenting of his repentance. Sometimes the importance of the future overwhelms him, and sometimes he feels that nothing is worth thinking of but the present. Such instability of sentiment must unsettle the believer. The man is sometimes as serene as a May morning, and sometimes as sweeping as a cyclone. You can never know how he will receive you, or how he will behave under certain circumstances. His instability imparts its changefulness to his countenance; while he is looking one way, his soul has gone another. His speech is ambiguous, his tones of voice wavering, his utterance now very rapid and now very slow. Sometimes he answers off-hand and without reflection, and then he requires so much time to consider, that the opportunity for speech has passed. He is untrustworthy in every department of life. That man "*can not*" receive anything of the Lord. He cannot hold his hand long enough to have anything placed therein.

SPECIFIC FORMS OF TROUBLE.

From a general discourse upon the variegated trials to which his brethren were exposed, and the design and joyful consummation of those trials, JAMES passes to specific cases, in which he gives specific exhortations and comforts.

The conditions of life are changeful. The poor may become rich, and the rich become poor; the lowly may be raised to the highest station, and the loftiest of mortals be cast to the ground. If a man have the Christian faith he may rejoice in either position, and may rejoice in passing from the one to the other.

And so JAMES says to his scattered parishioners and also to us, "*Let the brother of low degree rejoice in his exaltation, and the rich brother in his humbling, because he perishes like the flower of the grass: for the sun rose with a scorching wind and withered the grass, and the flower fell and the beauty of its appearance perished; thus also the rich man in his ways shall fade.*" (vv. 9, 10, 11.)

FROM LOW TO HIGH.

There are two senses in which the first clause may be taken, one of which seems much higher than the other. Let us first take that which is lower, namely, a poor brother passing into wealth. It is always to be remembered that he is our brother, no matter how little of this world's goods he may possess or control. It is a proper habit of thought to think always of all the poor as being our brothers. It is easy enough to claim kinship with the rich, but sometimes embarrassing to recognize consanguinity with the poor. But it is always noble to do so, even if the prospect be that our brother shall never accumulate any property. If it were not noble, even if it were not right, it would be prudent, as a man's financial condition never is an indication of his moral character, and as that financial condition may at any moment be suddenly and greatly changed. Emerson says, "Man was born to be rich, or inevitably grows rich by the use of his faculties, by the union of thought with nature. Property is an intellectual production. The game requires coolness, right reasoning, promptness and patience in the players. Cultivated labor drives out brute labor."

Sometimes a great accession of wealth comes suddenly, by the death of some rich kinsman, or a combination of circumstances which gives to a man's investments an unexpected increase of value. In this latter case he has wrought better than he knew. Let any man who has faith in God rejoice when this occurs. Let no man rejoice at such accession of riches if he be not the Lord's servant. "Rich and ungodly — a double hell-rope," exclaims Hedinger. But the good may rejoice because it has come to him in the providence of God. He has not set his heart inordinately upon it. It has come in the proper use of his faculties and opportunities.

Let him rejoice. Poverty has its trials as well as riches. He has endured the former, let him rejoice that he may now endure the latter. He has had the whole of the good effect of poverty, and now he is to have his discipline varied. He has suffered God's will, now he may do that will. He has been trained in the virtues which are passive, now he is to be trained in those which are active. He has often criticised the rich for not being more widely beneficent. Now, he has opportunity to set them an example, seeing that he has come into their rank, and has their opportunities. Yes, let him rejoice. He may not be able to do *more* good than he did in his former position; but he can do *other* good. But let him be careful, lest he begin to rejoice in the fact that he has now reached an estate in which he can gratify both in himself and in his family "the lust of the flesh, the lust of the eyes and the pride of life." But if he receive his wealth as a faithful and humble steward of his Lord, he *may* rejoice that his one talent has been made five.

FROM HIGH TO LOW.

"Oh, yes," says some one, "it is quite easy for the poor brother to rejoice in his exaltation; but how about the other brother? He has been brought low—well, let him also rejoice.

Has he employed his riches faithfully and well? Has he not made any of it to be "filthy lucre"? Has he used it as his Lord would have him use it? Then there can be no regrets. If it had remained with him, he would have continued the same course of conduct. There may be some Satan who said of him as was said of Job, "Doth Job serve God for nought?" Some bitter soul may have found his conduct so perfectly consistent that that could not be criticised, and so has said: "Oh, yes; it is very easy for *him* to serve God; he has all that heart could wish; he never had any financial cares; he never has to rack his brain to find where the next meal is to come from." God's grace is counted for nothing by such an observer. Now, the formerly rich brother can glorify God by showing that divine grace can sustain him as well in narrow and poor limits as it had done in large and wealthy places. Let the reduced brother rejoice.

Perhaps he has misused his wealth. Perhaps beyond a good and liberal living for himself and his family he has pampered them and hurt himself, and acquired such a love of gold as shuts out the love of God. He may have spent on himself what was meant for mankind. He may have been accumulating that which would have proved the ruin of his children.

Let the faithful as well as the unfaithful brother who has been brought from riches to poverty, rejoice; because (1) the change occurring in the providence of God, must be best for him; because (2) the ties that bound him to this world have been lessened and loosened; because (3) he has been relieved of a great responsibility; and because (4) in no case has he been robbed by the Lord, but in many senses he has been relieved by the Lord.

A HIGHER THOUGHT.

All this is a consideration of this passage on its lower ground of meaning. But there is manifestly a higher thought suggested, and one which probably was in the mind of JAMES, as well as that which we have been considering. It is this:

My brother, you are a Hebrew-Christian. You are a child of Abraham and a servant of Jehovah's Christ. You are of a low degree of glory, according to the world's estimation. You have no high political or social position, and you have no great wealth. But, yours is an exalted life. You are a child of Abraham and brother of Jesus. You have a light not "seen on sea or land"; an inner spiritual capability of discernment. You have also a spiritual power by which you are able to beat down Satan under your feet. You have a divine companionship, since Jehovah's Christ has promised that He will never leave you nor forsake you. You are now immortal; you have received that eternal life which is the gift of Jehovah through Jesus His Christ. When all the thrones, and crowns, and sceptres, and purples of all the monarchs now in power upon the face of the earth shall have gone to common dust, you will be reigning with Jehovah's Anointed in a kingdom which is not of this world. O brother of low degree, rejoice in your exaltation. To this great height you have been raised by your Christian faith. Your worldly position may always be low, but no power can deprive you of that spiritual exaltation which they have, and only they, whose life is hid with Christ in God.

THE FAITHLESS POOR CANNOT REJOICE.

The poor who have no faith, who do not belong to the brotherhood of God's spiritual family, have no reason to rejoice. While poverty is no disgrace, it certainly is no honor. It is a very great mistake to suppose that there is anything either ennobling or sanctifying in poverty. There are those who seem to believe that they must be happy in the next world because they have had so hard a time in this! But this is a grievous mistake. Afflictions make a man worse unless they be properly received and used. They work destruction of a sinner's peace and the degradation of his character. But, to a spiritual child of Abraham, brought into the family by Jesus the Christ, his affliction is "light," and "momentary," and "working" for him "more and more exceedingly an eternal weight of glory, while he is looking not at the things which are seen, but at the things which are not seen" (2 Cor. 4: 17).

THE FAITHLESS RICH CANNOT REJOICE.

In the same spirit JAMES addresses his rich brother, who is a Christian Israelite. If he were a sinner he would have no ground of rejoicing that his coffers were full, his money past count and his credit measureless. With all these, his separation from God, his lowness of character, and his certainty of final wreck, would take from him every ground of joy. Great riches are perilous. It has always been hard for a rich man to enter into the kingdom of heaven (Matt. 19: 23). Such a one never has entered that kingdom without God's special help of grace. Paul said (1 Tim. 6:9), "they that *determine* to be rich fall into ensnaring temptations and many senseless and ruinous longings, such as drown men in destruction and loss." That always takes place when he makes up his mind deliberately that he *will* be rich, that to that end all other things shall yield; personal culture, domestic enjoyment, public duties, being forced to stand aside until that end be reached.

But even if a man have not made that end paramount, if he have come to his great wealth by legitimate means or by inheritance, riches have the effect to make him self-dependent in a way which draws his faith from God, and self-exultant in a way which draws his love from his fellow-men.

Such a man should rejoice when he becomes a Christian, because the spirit of Christ which is in him will adorn his life with the beauty of humility, which is never so lovely as when seen in those whose condition militates against this grace. It will keep him from so fixing his affections upon material things as to draw him from spiritual culture. It will hold him to such a state of mind that if the summons come it will not tear him with anguish to part from that which he has made too large a part of his life. It will conform his life to that of our Master, who, though He was rich, yet for our sakes became poor, that we through His poverty might become rich (2. Cor. 8 : 9). He should rejoice in that religious faith which leads him to use the perishing properties of earth so as to transmute them into the enduring riches of eternity.

THE FAITHFUL RICH.

To his "brethren," to those who are in the faith, and are rich in that state of spiritual humility into which they have been brought by the Gospel does JAMES offer this ground of rejoicing: that they are delivered from the anxieties which torment other rich men, men who are never certain of retaining their earthly possessions; and those are the only riches such men have. They are no more secure of their position than the flowers of the fields. The very great suddenness of the change is indicated by the tenses JAMES employed. They had seen such flowers in all their morning glory. Suddenly, after the sun had risen, there had come a hot wind from the desert, and the beautiful flowers had fallen dishevelled to the ground. So familiar is the sight, that in all literature it has made a favorite figure with which to set forth the instability of earthly riches.

JAMES adds another, a figure employed by the Greek poet Æschylus, that of the drying up of a stream. The life of a rich man is like a flowing stream, which runs until the hot land through which it flows, drinks and drinks its waters, until the stream is dried up. Then all is gone.

Now, the believer, who in his riches is leading a holy, humble life, and steadily employing his wealth as the Master would have it, knows that he has a house not made with human hands, imperishable, secured in the heavens. (2 Cor. 5: 1.) If money, land, and other properties go, there abide with him the true riches which moth and rust cannot corrupt, and which thieves cannot steal.

We shall have frequent occasion to trace resemblances between the spoken words of Jesus and the written words of his brother JAMES. This is the first: Jesus (Matt. 5 : 3) said "Blessed are the poor in spirit, for theirs is the kingdom of the heavens." James wrote, "Let the brother of low degree of glory—let him shout—in his high estate."

HAPPINESS IN TRIALS.

Then, as if summing up in v. 12, JAMES states his theme—the happiness of such as show endurance *in temptation*—"*Happy the man who endures temptation, for being approved, he shall receive the crown of the life which the Lord has promised to those who love Him.*"

There are four possible experiences in regard to the trials of life. (1) They may fail of that which may be their best result. We may have the troubles of life—indeed, we *must* have them—and yet we may fail of the discipline. (2) They may be made seductions to evil and yielded to. (3) They may be suffered just as brutes suffer pain. (4) They may be "endured." Blessed is the man who has this last experience, who accepts the troubles of life as trials, who endures them, going on his way of duty as speedily in the storm as in the sunshine, obeying the injunction, "Let those who weep be as though they wept not." These are the blessed ones. There is no blessing for the untried man, as there is no currency for the unstamped bullion; for the metal, however precious, which is not marked so as to show that it has been tested and is now approved. There is no blessing for the man who yields to temptation or fails under trial. There is no blessing to him who has brutal insensibility to the pains of trial, or unconsciousness of the process, as the anvil is unconscious of the blows of the hammer. But there is a blessing for the man who knows what is going forward, who understands the intent, and appreciates the object, and desires the result of the process. For when he has become approved, after the testing and by reason of the testing, "*he shall receive the crown of the life.*"

It does not seem that this brilliant writer used his words carelessly. He does not say "diadem," which signifies kingly distinction, and which may fall by inheritance upon the brow of the meanest of men; but he says "crown," and uses a word which shows that the wearer has somehow been in conflict, and come out a conqueror. It is *that which has been won*. It is a mark of merit. It is not "a crown," but *the* crown. Crowns may fall and perish; but *the* crown is so enduring that others are scarcely worth mentioning. It is "the crown of *the* life." It is fadeless. The man that endureth temptation resembles that "blessed" man in Psalm 1, who is "like a tree planted by rivers of waters," whose "leaf shall not wither."

And the blessedness of wearing that crown shall be that it is given by the Lord. Anything is made more precious by being touched by Him. Now, He makes no mistake. Mortal judges of a contest may, through unconscious bias, or some unworthy motive, or through ignorance, or some other human infirmity, award the crown to the undeserving contestant; but the Lord never makes a mistake. He has promised it to a certain class, and He knows His own. Those who are to receive the crown are those who love Him, who have endured trial, not for anything which can gratify any low desires of their own, but out of love for Him. This is the secret of a blessed endurance. With the Lord, love is everything. There is no holy faith without love, no trustworthy hope, no worthy work. It is love that begets patience, and love for the Lord is so high and powerful that it enables a man to endure all things for Him. He has the constantly sustaining assurance that he loves the Lord, and the Lord loves him. What a happy man!

III.

The Temptation to Visionariness.

CHAPTER I., 13-17.

UNWORTHY THOUGHTS OF GOD.

JAMES now passes from external trials to the consideration of a condition of mind into which many souls are brought by those trials.

The word "temptation," we must keep in mind, bears the three meanings (1) of trials, (2) of evil suggestions, and (3) of seduction to sin. We all know how our trials work on our weak nature to draw us into the viciousness in which we represent God as the author of evils in which we indulge; evils spiritual and evils carnal. Do we exhibit weakness, irascibility, peevishness? How apt we are to say that if God had not allowed troubles to come upon us, we should never have indulged those ugly tempers. Does our faith fail, so that instead of holding to the right hand of His providence and seeking shelter in the bosom of His love, we resort to unchristian ways of taking care of ourselves? We charge God with driving us to this course. Do we lose relish for holy things, so that in our trouble we abandon the bread that cometh down from heaven, and strive to make our soul full by feeding it with husks of fleshly enjoyment? We defend ourselves to ourselves by charging God with driving us to this recourse. The consolations of God are small with us, and we are not content to say with holy Job, "Though He slay me, yet will I trust in Him." He hides His face from us, and we are not true to our covenant with Him; we are not willing to wait until the shadows pass away and He lift upon us the light of His countenance. We take ourselves to the baleful and lurid lights of our lusts; and we charge God with the result. Thus JAMES supposed that there might be those among his brethren in exile, who would say in their hearts that the unworthy thoughts of God and the temptation to apostatize which had come to them in the severe trials which they had endured, were to be laid at the door of God, and not charged to them.

Against yielding to this form of temptation, JAMES exhorts: "*Let no man say when he is seduced to evil that God is the seducer*" (v. 13).

THE ORIGIN OF EVIL.

The origin of evil has been the most puzzling riddle submitted to man's intellect from the first record of human thought down to this day. As God is the Eternal One, who existed before all things, and consequently before sin, men have always been prone to make Him the author of evil. "He foreknew all things, and He made all things. He must have foreseen that man would do wrong if created with a free will ; and yet He so created him. Does not that make God the author of evil?" That was the mode of reasoning of the ancient philosophers. The modern mode of reaching the same conclusion is somewhat after the following fashion : " A man's life is the result of his heredity and environment. He did not make his ancestors, and he did not choose his place in human society. God is responsible for both, and therefore responsible for the resulting sin."

NOT IN GOD.

JAMES prostrates both these arguments at a blow. The proper method of procedure is to endeavor to ascertain what kind of being God is, and then infer what kind of things He has done and will do. Find what your fountain is and you can determine its outflow. If you take the water as it is about to empty into the sea and analyze it, you cannot tell what it was as it burst from the fountain into the granite bowl up on the mountain-top. It has run through so much that was not clean granite, and has gathered into itself so much of such different things, that you cannot tell what it was at the fountain.

No. You cannot tempt God into being even a partner in your sin, in the most remote degree. God is untemptable and untempting. In His divine consciousness He has had no experience of sin, and in the forth-puttings of His divine activities He has never had any part or parcel in the suggestion of sin to others. As he is so holy that He can neither tempt nor be tempted in the bad sense, He must always be intending good ; as He is omniscient, He must always know what is the very best ; and as he is omnipotent, He must be able to carry it to the conclusions intended. We find man as God's creature. Whatever may surround that fact, we know that it is better that man should be simply because he is. As man has freedom of will, and could not exist as man without freedom of will, we know that it is best that there should be freedom of will in man. No ; without absurdity, we cannot think of God as the author of sin.

Nor is it possible to conceive of a world in which there should be existing *two* intelligent, moral beings, that is, beings having relationship and consequently ethical possibilities, without the possible existence of sin ; because sin is a violation of relations, and the existence of one man and of one God would institute relationships which would create obligations. Virtue consists in the exercise of the will to choose to meet and discharge all duties produced by obligation. But if a man can choose such a course as that, he can also choose the opposite. And that opposite is evil.

IN THE INDIVIDUAL.

Thus JAMES gives us the genesis of evil. It is in the individual man. The man is drawn away from good and caught in evil by his own lust. The writer lays special emphasis on this: it is "*his own;*" it is not of God; it is not of the devil; it is not of the world; it is of the man's self and in the man's self. It is that in his soul without the exhibition of which there would be nothing to which the work of the devil could appeal. It is most important to perceive and believe this; it is most important to inculcate·in all children that it is a mistake to lay their faults on any one else, even on the devil. That personage has enough to bear without having our sins laid upon him. No sinner can be reformed so long as he makes Satan or any one else responsible for his transgressions. I knew a child of strong character and strong passions, who used to have paroxysms of rage. Her parents and others would sometimes tell her to open her mouth and let the bad spirit go under the table. The child was growing into the belief that she was the innocent victim of an unseen being, who was another person, and she was learning to shift all the responsibility upon that person, that person not herself. A friend one day taught her the fallacy of this; showed her that she was the only person responsible; that she herself was the bad spirit, and there was nothing to do but have that spirit, namely, herself, totally changed. She went to her closet and prayed — prayed as King David prayed (Ps. 51) when the conviction seized him that it was against God, and God only, that he had sinned. His cry rang with "*my* trangressions," "*my* iniquity," "*my* sin." There was no third party in the transaction. From the hour the child had that conviction, she was a changed person.

So must we all feel. We can never resist temptation as we should, so long as we hold God or any one else responsible for *our* sins.

HEREDITY.

There is such a thing as heredity. That is perfectly well settled. There is an inherited depravity of nature in every man. You have it. Run your eye along the line of your depravity both ways. It came from your parents, and theirs from their ancestors. Some one must be responsible. If our ancestors had resisted, the taint might have been eliminated or modified. No one of them was guilty because he inherited it; but he was guilty for any increase thereof which he sent down to his descendants. So will you and I be if we do not fight with all the weapons and aids in our reach against the seductions to sin.

Men seem sometimes to forget the obvious truth that heredity is a line which does not stop at them. If they recollected this truth perhaps they would resist sin more strenuously. Many a man says, "Well, it's in my blood, as my grandfather's gluttony is in my gout. I can't help it. There's no use trying." And in that temper he throws himself heedlessly upon all ways of sinning. And so the next generation has increased depravity. But God has no responsibility in this matter.

ENVIRONMENT.

In like manner we must consider our environment. Every man must be born somewhere. He must have father and mother. He cannot exist without some environment. It is impossible to conceive of any environment which may not appeal to a human being in the way of seduction to evil. Therefore, no man must lay his sin to his environment, and through that to God. His environment all the more evil it is, calls upon him all the more loudly for a virtuous battle against that which appeals to him to draw him into sin. God cannot be held responsible if the man do not make the effort to be virtuous.

Let it be understood, then, by us all and forever, that God never puts before us or around us anything intended by Him to influence us to do wrong. Let us pull up that bad thought by the roots. Let us never for a moment give place to the suggestion that by those decrees and arrangements by which the world was made and goes forward, God has arranged things so that there must be sin sometime, somewhere, by somebody. Even when others tempt us, sometimes those very near to us and dear to us, as our husbands, or our wives, or our parents, or our children, our pastors or intimate Christian friends, when it seems as if God might have prevented it, but by allowing it, becomes responsible; even when there are a thousand things which cannot be explained, some of them very torturing to a sensitive Christian; under all circumstances, let us remember that one thing has been settled most thoroughly and forever by the explicit declaration, *God cannot be tempted with evil, neither tempteth He any man.*

THE GENESIS OF EVIL.

No; the source of the evil is in us. JAMES gives the genesis of it. His psychology is that of St. Paul and of the New Testament generally. A man is spirit, soul and body. The real personality of the man is his spirit. There is his permanent identity. There is his emperorship; for in the spirit is the will. The body is the spirit's home and the spirit's instrument of communication with the outer world, that world which has the qualities of matter. The soul is the connecting link between the body and spirit. In the soul are the desires for the things which are known by the senses. It is here that JAMES finds the origin of evil. Desire is quite innocent in its normal conditions. It becomes excited under the influence of the things in the outward world; of those things of which it has knowledge in the body, or by means of the body. If those things are according to the will of God and the desire solicits, and secures the consent of the spirit, then the indulgence of the senses produces that which is good. But if the desire is stirred toward that which is contrary to the will of God and it proceeds to solicit the spirit, without whose consent nothing can be done, and succeeds in gaining the consent of the spirit, then comes sin.

"DRAWN AWAY" AND "ENTICED."

Such seems to be the psychologic basis of JAMES'S argument. Then he describes the genesis and progress of sin. "*But each man is tempted by his own lust, when he is being drawn away by it and enticed*" (v. 14). It is a powerful picture which he paints. Desire is represented as a harlot soliciting the spirit to an impure embrace. This harlot's arts are represented under two words, taken from hunting and fishing. As the hunter draws his game from some safe covert, as the fisherman baits his hook and catches the fish, so the harlot employs allurements to draw away the solicited person from all those protections to his innocency which might save him, that she may then overcome him with her blandishments.

It is well to pause for profitable self-application of this great truth. We cannot be "enticed" until "drawn away." Let every fish keep to his cover. Let no man rush into temptation. Let none of us go into "doubtful places," by which phrase we ought to understand not simply those places which are *known to be dangerous*, but also those places which are *not known to be safe*. Let our society be chosen of those who are known to be pure and wholesome, not of those whose influence over us is uncertain.

COMPANIONS AND AMUSEMENTS.

How much would be saved in our ordinary life if this rule were observed! If, in our every-day table-life, we used such food in such quantities as we know to be wholesome, and avoided every article of diet of whose effect upon our stomachs we were doubtful, how much physical and mental suffering we should avoid! If, in the choice of our companions, we associated only with such persons as we knew to be good, and forsook all those whose characters were merely dubious, how many disagreeable and injurious complications we should escape! If, in the choice of our books we selected only such as were known to be absolutely unexceptionable in moral tone, while good in literary style, how much corruption of the imagination, and soiling of the soul, and pain of conscience we should be spared!

Let the same rule be applied everywhere. The question of amusements and other enjoyments often arises, especially with young Christian people. It is the glittering fly thrown into the water by the skilful angler. Its brilliant colors can do no harm to the fish that stays away from it. Let the young man confine himself to such amusements as no one suspects of being harmful and he is safe.

It goes without saying that every man must be amused; that is, drawn away from strenuous thought, so that he may return fresher to that work which is necessary. If a man were so constituted that he could maintain the mental and bodily exercise necessary for the discharge of those duties on which his own welfare depends, as well as the welfare of others, for him there would be no need of amusement. The necessity for *its* existence lies in the necessity for serious thought, which cannot be kept in endless continuity. We have not the word "musement" in the English language as a synonyme for "serious thought." If we had, then its opposite word would be "*a*musement," as one's "*a*vocation" is that which calls him off from his "vocation," which is his regular calling in life. Whatsoever, then, rests a man, leaves him in the best condition of body, soul, and spirit, to return to the discharge of the duties of life, that is the amusement which he can indulge with perfect impunity. When anything else is offered, let him remember the fisherman's arts, copied by the harlot, and used by JAMES to describe the first part of the journey to destruction.

THE PLAN OF THE SEDUCER.

Is it not always the plan of a soul-destroyer to draw his victim from a safe retreat? Does the gambler, the conspirator, or the harlot ever go up into your home, and enter the apartment, where you are sitting between your venerable mother and your pure sister, near the paternal hearthstone, and "entice" you, endeavoring there and then to induce you to engage in open wickedness? Never. But the first arts of one who seeks you for a partner in guilt are to draw you away from your moral defences, knowing how easily a small party can resist a great force attacking a well-fortified castle, a party which in an open field would be instantly overwhelmed by the superior army.

So men are often drawn from the bulwark of the light into the defencelessness of darkness. You may walk with a measure of safety through any city during the day; but the social beasts of prey, like those of the forests, walk forth in the night. It would save the young men who go to large cities, and old men as well, if they made the rule to keep their confidence, and even their company, from strangers who address them. A man is safe so long as he stays in his hotel, and hears what any stranger has to say, but allows the stranger to know nothing about himself or his affairs. He is on the way to trouble when he commits himself to any strange man on the street, to be led he knows not whither. He is on the highway to destruction if he allow himself to hold any conversation with any "strange woman" he may meet on the street. The "strange woman" has been the person to be avoided from the days of Solomon to this day.

"Drawn away!" That is the first danger. Drawn away from the father's counsel, drawn away from the mother's influence, drawn away from the sanctuary of the church service, drawn away from the sanctities of the Lord's Day, drawn away from the teaching of the Holy Scriptures. Whoever takes the first step does not find it difficult to take the next and the next, and whosoever takes those few steps cannot be far from the destruction of all those things which are most valuable to a man. There is almost no difficulty in "enticing" a man who has been "drawn away."

A HORRIBLE PICTURE.

But if the man allow himself to be drawn away and enticed, something dreadful will follow. *"Then Desire, having conceived, brings forth Sin, and Sin completed becomes pregnant with death"* (vv. 15, 16).

What a frightful picture JAMES paints. Desire has successfully solicited the will to an impure embrace. In the unblessed union the child, Sin, is conceived and finally brought forth. It is a little one. It may be as pretty and as playful as a tiger's kitten. But it grows. When Sin, which is so vigorous, has attained its growth it becomes a dreadful parent, and its fearful offspring is Death. Before a man sins let him consider this tremendous genealogy. The sinner is the father of his own sin and the grandfather of his own death. It is all inside himself. It is not of God ; it is not of God !

Whatever may have been JAMES's special thought and intention as towards his Hebrew brethren, however much he may have endeavored to warn them against that road which leads to complete and final apostasy, the lesson to us is plain. Sin continued grows stronger and stronger by habit, until it has obtained such dominion of us as to strangle the spirit and thus make a complete wreck of the whole man. So, while JAMES is endeavoring to save us from having wrong thoughts of God, as if providential trials were temptations in the bad sense, according to the Rabbinical metaphor, he thrills us with a stirring warning against the dangerous, the ruinous nature of sin, which at first may be like a spider's web, but afterwards becomes a strong cable.

Having done this, he returns to the correction of the error into which we are prone to fall. That correction he finds in setting before us the opposite truth. So far is God from being the author of evil, He is the only author of any good,

He is the author of all good; there is no good which does not proceed from God, as certainly as there is no evil which does not have its origin outside of God.

A GREAT ERROR.

"*Do not err, my brethren beloved,*" says our author, v. 16; do not wander away from the truth as to the essential nature of God.

It may be well to consider the verse as being more than a mere rhetorical call to something very important which the writer had to say. It does that most effectually, but it does something more. It emphasizes the importance of having correct views of God. In regard to other things, wander into the forests of falsehood so far as one may, the man who holds the truth as to God can never be finally lost. And yet how few seem to appreciate that. Any philosophy of physical science is unsound and untrustworthy in proportion to its holding unsound relations to the truth as to God. The same is true in civil life: no man can attain to the loftiest statesmanship, whose principles of government are not in harmonious accord with the truth as to God. It is equally true in the religious life: heresies in doctrine, errors in morals, and wrongs in life are to be traced almost invariably to some mistake of the truth as to God. Let a man be right here, and he has found a hasp on which he may hang the first link of any chain of thought or action or life which he may be able to forge in time and in eternity. Do not wander from the great central truth as to God.

A GREAT TRUTH.

And this is that great central truth.

"*Every gift that is good, and every perfect endowment is from above, coming down from the Father of lights.*" No man has anything good which has been produced by his own nature. All good is from outside. That is the first part of the truth. JAMES employs in this sentence the very word which Jesus used in speaking to Nicodemus in regard to the new birth (John 3 : 3), "begotten *from above.*" It teaches the truth that there is no such thing as spontaneous regeneration. So, His brother JAMES teaches that there is no such thing as spontaneous goodness among men. If there be anything good in the universe, enjoyed by men or beasts, or any other thing living in heaven or on earth, visible or invisible, it is the gift of God. If it be a transient good, enjoyed and then gone, so that nothing but the memory of the enjoyment is left, it is the gift of God. If it be the fountain of a stream rolling out pleasure or power to irrigate the world, it is the gift of God. The universe may be searched. If anywhere anything can be found which any intellect can perceive, and any heart can feel to be good, it has come from God. If it be good for any man's body, good for any man's soul, good for any man's spirit, if it be good for any other animal, if it be good for the present or future inhabitants of the earth—find a good thing, and you find a Godsend.

Among the good things, the best is light, the physical light which makes the things of the outer world visible, the intellectual light which enables any man to see truths and their relations, the spiritual light which enables a man to walk as seeing Him that is invisible and the invisible world by which He is surrounded. God is the Father of "lights," the source of all conceivable modes of illumination, and He pours down upon men all the good things they have. It is not a shower, an occasional gift of things desirable, but it is an unceasing rain of blessings. It is incessant sunshine. As at all hours rays of light are going off in all directions from the sun, and covering all the space of the solar system, so are God's gifts going from Him, descending from Him, ceaselessly, in an unbroken stream of blessing and an uninterrupted radiation of light.

THE FATHER OF LIGHTS.

He is the Father of lights, the producer of the heavenly bodies, the source of all the light of knowledge, all the light of wisdom, all the light of faith, all the light of hope, all the light of love, all the light of joy. If any man arise in his generation to shine as a star in the hemisphere of human society, God kindled the splendor of his intellect and the benign radiance of his high spiritual character. If any woman arise to brighten a home, or send the kindly light of her sweetness over any cheerless portion of our race, it was God who dwelt in her heart, and smiled through her life. If on the coast of our humanity, we, mariners on life's uncertain sea, behold light-houses so placed along the shore as to enable us to take bearings and shape courses that bring us to our havens of safety, it is God who has erected each such light-house and kindled each such pharos.

The world can never cease being grateful for Moses, and David, and Paul; for Homer, and Plato, and Shakespeare; for Copernicus, Kepler, and Newton; for Jerome, and Luther, and Wesley — the great lights of philosophy, poetry and piety. It must be remembered that none of these came of themselves; that they were all kindled by the Father of lights. The great light which inwardly "enlighteneth every man that cometh into the world" is a light that streams from God. And He who dared to declare of Himself what no one has yet shown to be untrue, "I am the light of the world; he that followeth Me shall not walk in darkness, but shall have the light of life"—He was the Son of God.

All through human society at this day we find followers of Jesus—men "blameless and harmless, the sons of God, without rebuke, in the midst of a crooked and perverse nation, among whom they shine as lights in the world " (Phil. 2:15), and we know that they are not the product of any malevolent spirit ; we know that they themselves did not produce the light which shineth in them ; we know that for them we are indebted to God, who calls Himself "the Father of Lights."

THE CHANGELESS FATHER.

Of this God, who is the giver of every transient gift which is good, and every permanent endowment which is valuable, JAMES says : "*With whom there is not existing a change or shadow-casting.*" He took his metaphor from nature. His readers would immediately think of the sun, the ruler of the solar system. And that would remind them of the very obvious phenomena of the sun's declinature to the south and return to the north, as the seasons succeed one another, and the alternations of day and night. If these suggested any mutability, or variability or inconstancy in God, anything indeed which might weaken our faith, he adds that God is not only the giver of every good and perfect gift, but He is also without variableness or shadow-making. It is not necessary to press the astronomical figures which he employs. It is clear that he means to assert most emphatically two things about God, namely, that with Him there is no *alienation* of goodness and no *obscuration* of goodness. As one says, "God is always in the meridian."

Of such a God it would be absurd to suppose that He could be the author of evil or the tempter of His mortal children. Any logical processes which landed a mind on that proposition may thence be inferred to be illegitimate and vicious.

IV.

The New Life versus Fanaticism.

CHAPTER I., 18–27.

REGENERATION.

JAMES presses upon his readers the idea of God's invariable goodness in another form. He appeals to their experience in regeneration. In proof of the proposition that God, the Father of lights, cannot do evil but good, always and in every direction, there was the fact of their own conversion to Christianity, and their spiritual new-birth. "*According to His free determination He hath brought us forth, by the word of His truth, that we should be a kind of first-fruit of His creatures*" (v. 18).

Here is a splendid specimen of God's good gifts, in that He has given us eternal life through His Son Jesus. This life is the climax of divine goodness, as Death, the child of sin, is the climax of human badness. It was free. It came by no law, it was produced by no necessity, it was the product of no natural evolution, it arose from His own goodness and lovingness. He emphasizes "us" in addressing Hebrew-Christians. They were originally chosen by His divine goodness to be the repository of the oracles of God, the ark, so to speak, which should bear the truth of God down the stream of the centuries. When the fulness of time had come, and Jesus inaugurated the ripened plans for the world's salvation, those Israelites who earliest became Christians, had the distinction of being a kind of first-fruits of all God's creatures. Christianity had completed to them the revelation that under God the highest beings are men, that humanity is to take the lead of the universe, that men are superior to angels, and men are to live forever, and are to lead and govern and teach the intelligences of the universe, that those individuals of humanity who are to do this, are those who receive eternal life through Jesus Christ, and that the first, as the first-fruits of an abundant harvest, are those Jews who were early in Christ, having been begotten by the word of truth.

It is as if he had said to them, "Think of it, brethren. Poor, unknown, despised, both among the Gentiles and in your own nationality, you are heirs of God and joint-heirs with Christ Jesus. Born children of Abraham, ye have been reborn brothers of Jesus. Whoever else may by any process of thought be betrayed into accounting God the author of evil, you never can. To you He must ever be the Giver of every good gift, physical, intellectual, spiritual, temporal and eternal."

FANATICISM.

JAMES now passes to an admonition to his brethren against *fanaticism* as another form of temptation. He proceeds: "*Let every man be swift to hear, slow to speak, slow to wrath; for the wrath of man does not work the righteousness of God. Wherefore, removing all impurity, and all outflowing, in meekness receive the ingrafted word, the thing which is able to save your souls. But, become doers of the word and not hearers only, deluding your own selves. For, if any one is a hearer of the word and not a doer, he is like unto a man observing his natural face in a mirror, for he observed himself, and he hath gone away, and he forgot what sort of a man he was. But he who becomes absorbed in the completed law, the law of liberty, and continues, not a hearer that forgets, but a doer who works, this man shall be blessed in his doings.*"

The well-known wisdom of swiftness to hear and slowness to speak, has been inculcated by teachers in all ages. On his disciples Pythagoras enjoined five years of preliminary silence. It was supposed that such a long probation in which there should be total abstinence from speech would give the disciple the advantage of hearing much and hearing it attentively; because the mind was not preoccupied with preparing and uttering an answer. There was supposed to be also the other advantage of pondering what was heard; so that it should be well marked and thoroughly digested. Some one has called attention to the fact, that a man has two ears and but one tongue, and inferred therefrom that a man ought to hear at least twice as much as he speaks.

SWIFT TO HEAR AND SLOW TO SPEAK.

As touching the matter of which JAMES had been writing to his brethren, namely, their troubles and the temptations likely to arise therefrom, this admonition was most timely. They should be swift to hear. God, who had spoken to Elijah in the still small voice, was now speaking to them in their great trials. God is talking. He may speak slowly. We must "wait God's leisure." We must be attentive to the voice in the darkness, as little Samuel was to the night-voice in the Temple. "God is His own interpreter;" but He never hurries; with Him a thousand years are as a day.

And so we must be slow to speak; very slow to make our own interpretation; and slower in making charges against God. If we speak incontinently, we shall not only be indiscreet, but we shall excite ourselves to anger. The tongue kindles.

See what folly it is to be angry against God for His providences. Do we know what God is doing? Does not God know all things? Can He not relieve? And will He not relieve at the proper time and in the proper manner? See what a sin it is: that great, black sin of ingratitude. Has not every good gift enjoyed by us come from Him? What led Him to the bestowment of those gifts? Was not the motive wholly in Him? Does He ever change? Is he not the same? Whatsoever, therefore, comes from Him must be good.

It is well to regulate our lives by the great precept, "Swift to hear, slow to speak, slow to wrath," because of the injurious effect upon others of a failure to be guided thereby. Our circle of relatives and friends know how quick to advance opinions are those who are either ignorant or half-taught. If they discover that we are impatient of the speech of others, are unwilling to hear what may be said upon the other side, they will perceive in us an unchristian lack of charity for others as well as the absence of that modesty which always accompanies wisdom. If they find that we have an off-hand opinion upon all the gravest questions which concern God and man, upon the most mysterious problems of the universe, they will lose respect for our utterances, and our influence over them for good will depart. If we are not slow to anger, it will exhibit such a want of self-control as will deprive us of the power of governing others.

SLOW TO WRATH.

Haste in thought or speech tends to anger, as the wise man knew when he said, "Be not hasty in thy spirit to be angry" (Eccl. 7 : 9). To be angry with the truth is quite as much a folly as a sin, and so is it to be angry with those who tell us the truth. The king of Israel was a contemptible person when he declined to send for Macaiah, and said of him to the king of Judah, "I hate him, for he doth not prophesy good of me, but evil" (1 Kings 22 : 8). Jonah was not a bad man, he was a prophet of the Lord, yet the Lord's merciful dealings with Nineveh displeased him, because it seemed to disparage his prophetic authority. "It displeased Jonah exceedingly, and he was very angry" (Jonah 4 : 1). His anger threw a cloud over all his character, and over all his previous life, and over the first missionary enterprise undertaken on the planet. We leave Jonah with a sort of contempt, as the curtain drops over the picture of Jehovah's remonstrating with him, and saying, "Doest thou well to be angry for the gourd," and Jonah's peevish reply, "I do well to be angry, even unto death," and the Lord's grandeur, His wide goodness, as He says, "Thou hast spared the gourd for the which thou hast not labored, neither madest it grow, which came up in a night and perished in a night; and should not I spare Nineveh, that great city wherein are more than six score thousand persons that cannot discern between their right hand and their left hand, and also much cattle?" Let us remember that anger against

God is anger against infinite and eternal love, and to indulge it is to make a copartnership with Satan.

Moreover, the wrath of man does not work out the righteousness of God, either in ourselves or in others. There is no regulative force in anger as there is in love. Anger is zeal gone crazy. JAMES knew that his brethren were apt to be angry in theological and ecclesiastical discussions. He warns them that no good would come of such heat. They did not all take his advice. Some still held that men could be brought by passionate appeals to see the truth as they saw it. The result was the Jewish war. Mahomet thought the same, and so drew the sword. Christian sects have pursued the same course towards one another. Where there have been no unsheathed swords and no kindled fagots and no material instruments of bodily torture, there has been fierce wrath in controversy and terrible denunciations and social pains and penalties; but never yet, since the world began, has the wrath of man worked the righteousness of God.

Epigrammatic as much of JAMES'S writings are, there is in them a continuity of thought well worth studying. His brother, Jesus, in the memorable intercessory prayer which He offered to His Father, just before His departure from His disciples, indicated the instrument of human sanctification; "Sanctify them through the truth; Thy word is truth." (John 17 : 17.) When JAMES is instructing and guiding his brethren, he guards them against allowing their troubles to become temptations, in the sense of seductions to evil, and, in case they sinned, he warned against the additional sin of laying their wrong-doing at the door of God. That led him to a description of the genesis of evil; and that to a description of the genesis of holiness. God begets us unto righteousness of His own will (masculine), with the word of truth (feminine) (v. 18).

A PREPARATION OF HEART.

That the word of God may have full power over us, there must be a preparation of heart for its reception. We must cease to do evil before we can learn to do well. We must lay aside everything which is offensive to the purity of God. By the term "filthiness" JAMES seems to wish to arouse a sense of the loathsomeness of all sin. He does not simply mean that we shall lay aside those particular sins which are disgusting to us; but rather to impress us that all sin has in it that which makes it disgusting to God. He may here be supposed to be thinking of sins of the flesh, the visible violations of the moral law. Then we are to lay aside all "superfluity of naughtiness," as our Common Version has it. That does not mean that there is a measure of sin we may retain, but we must draw the line somewhere. The word translated "superfluity" signifies "an outflowing." The same word occurs in Romans 5 : 15, and 2 Cor. 8 : 2. It is a New Testament word, and indicates that which goes out to others. Here it means the outflowing of malice. By the one phrase JAMES may be supposed to refer to sins of the flesh, and by the other sins of the spirit. While indulging ourselves either in sins which others cannot see, or sins which show themselves in displays of evil temper, we cannot profit by the word of God.

Meekness, as well as purity, is essential to the proper hearing of the word of God. One cannot in private approach the study of the word in the pride of opinion or of scholarship, nor can one resort to the word for the purpose of sustaining one's own dogma, and while in that spirit find the word profitable. You know that this is sometimes done. A man may take down the Bible to find proof passages, just as a lawyer may search the Reports of the Supreme Court to find only that which will sustain his theory of the case which he is to try. In such search he throws aside whatever does not make for his side. He is not learning law, he is hunting helps. If the Bible be so studied it will be improfitable. We must approach it with the docility of little children (Matt. 18 : 23). We must simply wish to learn what is the mind of the Spirit in the word of God.

LISTENING TO PREACHING.

In that spirit men must listen to preaching. They must not love to hear only that which suits their fancies, their tastes, or their opinions. In seeking a preacher their one inquiry should be for the man who can most edifyingly unfold to them the word of the Lord. It may hurt, in the sense of giving pain; but so may a needed surgical operation. Growing angry with the surgeon is not promotive of any good to the patient. So, all malice must be put out of the heart if the word of the Lord is to have free course and be glorified.

The sins of the flesh and of the spirit must be put away, so far as we have power to do it, that the word of God may be ingrafted in us. Wherever grafting is known, this is an impressive phrase. The tree is cut open that the new shoot may be inserted.

The first lesson is a recurrence of what we have already been taught, namely, that that which saves a man "comes from the outside." No manner or amount of culture which a man can give himself will save that man by making him holy, any more than anything which the wild apple-tree can do for itself, will turn it into the producer of the best kinds of apples. It is always from without. It is not cultivation men need so much as regeneration. In the spiritual it is as in the material: Life is always from without. Nothing has ever been known to beget itself.

THE INGRAFTED WORD.

The second lesson is that our only hope of salvation is the having the word of God ingrafted in our spirits. This makes the whole subject tremendously solemn. The destruction of the soul is that which results from the failure to have the word of God so in us that we share its nature.

But, it is indispensable that we be doers of the word, not hearers only. The man who supposes that all that is necessary is that he run over a passage of Holy Scripture before leaving his bed-chamber, and another at family prayer, and give respectful attention to his clergyman in synagogue or church, is greatly mistaken. He must work out in life what he reads or hears from the Holy Scripture, as the sap of a tree works out fruit on the stem which is grafted thereon. It is the failure to do this which has so greatly retarded our religious life. Men have heard the word with their outward ears, and have gone out of the church thinking that the sermon was done, whereas it had not begun in their practice, not even in their hearts.

No; the moment I have learned anything from the word I must make a strenuous effort to reproduce *it* in my life. Then, the next thing learned; then, the rest; and so on, until my life be an incarnation of the Bible. If each hearer did this how powerful our holy faith would be among men! Compared with this what is success in controversy, although I could silence every theological opponent? What Biblical learning, although I could repeat every verse of the Bible in every tongue ever spoken among men? Neither of these would save me; but the truth, animated unto fruitage by my spiritual vitality, would make me a tree worth a place in God's orchard. What kind of people are those who hear but fail to practise? They are like a man who sees his face in a mirror, perhaps while shaving, and after he has gone, cannot reproduce to his memory any accurate picture of the countenance which he had seen. So, the hearers who are non-doers carry away a vague idea of their spiritual character. It does them no good. It is this vagueness which is so injurious to the mass of gospel hearers. The preacher who can print something distinct upon the minds of his people can be of real service to them. They must be arrested, shaken, roused, stimulated, spurred, stung, until they feel the indispensableness of turning from less important things to give themselves to the study of the word of God.

THE LAW OF LIBERTY.

JAMES paints a companion picture to that of the man who glances at a mirror. It is that of a man who bends himself to—who becomes absorbed in—the law, the completed law, the system of religion which began with Abraham and was completed by Jesus. The incomplete law set forth by Moses, can only show him just what he is, as a mirror shows a man his face. Even if a man bow himself to that, and become absorbed in that, it only shows how bad he is, and even the most vigorous effort to keep that law only more and more demonstrates to him what a slave he is to his sinfulness. But, the law which is completed in Jesus is the law o liberty; that law which is the Gospel of redemption frees a man from the guilt of his committed sins and from the power of his native sinfulness.

But, he must be constantly obedient thereto. It is not a mere passing glance that is required. He must inspect it closely, and meditate upon it deeply, and obey it constantly. Jesus said (John 14:21), "He that hath My commandments and *keepeth* them, he it is that loveth Me; and he that loveth Me shall be loved of My Father, and I will love him, and will manifest Myself to him"; and (John 18:31) "if the Son shall make you free, ye shall be free indeed." It was the mistake of the Jew of JAMES'S day that he believed a knowledge of the law was saving. Against this error Paul teaches when he says (Romans 1:13), "For not the hearers of the law are righteous before God, but the doers of the law shall be accounted righteous." And so Jesus said of those who abode in Him and in whom His words abode, that they should glorify His Father, and bear much fruit, and *so* be His disciples (John 15).

Such a man shall be blessed "in his doing." Remark that the reward of happiness is not to come to him *for* his deed, and is not in the future. The blessedness is in the very act. We need not seek blessedness; we must practise obedience, and then the blessedness comes of itself. Who that has set himself to doing all that the Lord commands has not found that it made life, even a life of self-sacrifice, more delicious than all carnal delight?

A MISTAKE AS TO RELIGION.

JAMES then points out to his Jewish-Christian brethren a distinction between false and true religion, which is just as good for our age as for his. *"If among you any man fancies himself religious, not leading his tongue with a bridle, but cheating his own heart, this man's religion is useless."*

Whether there was some special reason why JAMES should call the attention of his Hebrew-Christian brethren to sins of the tongue we do not know; but we do know that if ever a generation needed repeated and pungent reminders on this subject, ours is that generation. Perhaps, also, he felt as if some might restrict what he had just said to *acts*, and he desired to let them know that they must include *words* as well. Moreover, the Jews in the time of Christ were misled by the belief that professions were sufficient, so that if any man read and taught the law, especially if he taught it, he would inevitably be saved, whatever might be the moral character of his life. JAMES'S brother Jesus found that sentiment so powerful among His disciples, that He was compelled to warn them that it was not those who made loud professions that were to be saved. Almost the last thing He said in His memorable discourse called the " Sermon on the Mount," was to lift a warning against that form of self-deception which was founded on mere profession. "Not every one that *saith unto Me* 'Lord, Lord,' shall enter into the kingdom of heaven, but he that doeth the will of My Father in heaven" (Matt. 7 : 21). And the words which next follow are tremendous: "*Many* will say to Me in that day, 'Lord, Lord, have we not prophesied in Thy name? and in Thy name have cast out devils? and in Thy name done many wonderful works?' And then will I profess to them, I never knew you; depart from Me ye that work iniquity."

We must not be deceived by our own professions. If any member of our body be an instrument of sin it shows that our hearts are still unconquered by the grace of God. And no member more quickly shows this than the tongue. And few things are more injurious than an unbridled tongue. A fool's tongue wanders everywhere, into fields lawful and unlawful. Men have no right to talk heedlessly. It is no excuse that a speaker did not mean to do wrong, or that he "meant nothing by it." We are bound to mean something every time we speak, and we are bound to mean something good; the tongue must have on the bridle of thought, and that must be held by the reason, which is the right hand of religion. It is of those words which were not intended by the speaker to be profitable, words uttered when he "meant nothing," that Jesus said : "I say unto you that every idle word that men shall speak, they shall give account thereof in the day of judgment" (Matt. 12 : 36)

It may be a question which does most harm, a false tongue or an unbridled tongue. In the case of the former, it may so soon be discovered that it is the instrument of a liar that all men can guard themselves against it ; but the unbridled tongue may belong to a man who has some pleasing qualities, or to a woman who but for her wild tongue would be a charming person, and so people are thrown off their guard, and the secret poison of the bitter and bad word may work disastrously.

The man who professes to be a believer and possesses an unbridled tongue, is utterly useless to the cause of all true religion. He may be very punctual in attendance upon all forms of public worship ; he may even take part in them, exhibiting great gifts in prayer and great zeal for religion ; he may be a very genial and companionable person, witty and bright ; he may seem to take great interest in others, and give of his own income or substance to promote what are considered the interests of religion ; all that and much more may he do ; with the industry of a gambler striving to cheat from himself the verdict that he is a truly religious man ; and yet all the while that man's religion may be as empty as a bubble, vain and unprofitable to others and unhelpful to himself ; idle, foolish, useless, trifling, thoughtless, wanton, irreverent, profane, for the word translated "idle" means all these things.

RELIGION IS IN CHARACTER.

JAMES teaches us that the proof of religion is not in mere profession, but in character, and therefore a man cannot by words prove to himself, or to his fellow-man, that he is religious ; the proof is in his actions. His brother Jesus had said, "By their fruits ye shall know them" (Matt. 7 : 20).

"*Religion, clear and spotless, toward God, even the Father, is this : to keep guardianship over orphans and widows in their affliction, to keep one's self stainless from the world*" (v. 27).

It is necessary to notice that the writer is not giving us a definition of religion, but a description ; a description of its character by showing something which it will do outwardly, something it will produce which we shall be able to see. It were a great mistake to consider this an authoritative, scientific definition of religion. The writer had been pointing out the marks of a useless religion. He now indicates the characteristics of any religion which is pure and spotless. Indeed, it might be written "*any* religion," which God sees to be pure and spotless, will have the characteristics of outward beneficence and inward purity.

By a beautiful figure, he likens religion to a gem, a precious stone, the value of which depends upon the two qualities of (1) being clear through and through, without any inner malformation, and (2) being free from all stain or flaw on the outside. Positively, and as to its interior, it is clear and unclouded; negatively, and as to its exterior, it is spotless and flawless. Any religion which has these qualities is a true religion, and will produce purity and usefulness; and, whatever its pretensions, a religion destitute of these, is worthless.

Let us notice how JAMES turns this subject Godward, whereas the general disposition is to turn it manward. It is not of such importance to me that men consider me religious; they may be mistaken. Nor, that I consider myself religious; I may be mistaken, may even deceive myself. But God cannot be mistaken or deceived. That religion which, in His judgment, is clear and spotless, which presents no cloudiness and no flaw to His inspection, is the religion that is worth thinking about. Indeed, the phrase which we have translated "toward God," and which the Common Version gives "before God," strictly means "in the judgment of God."

A LIFE OF BENEFICENCE.

A truly religious life is a life of beneficence. It does not consist alone in creeds and opinions, although it could not exist without them. It is built on a religion which looks outward more than inward. The subject thereof is careful for the rights and welfare of others, not spending his whole time and force on himself in morbid study of his interior spiritual conditions and experiences. It is an indication that the man is a child of God when he bears the family likeness. The children are like the Father, and much the larger part of the revelation which God makes of Himself is not what God thinks of Himself or does for Himself, but what He thinks of others and does for others. He represents Himself as beginning farthest off from Himself, and taking first under His special divine care those who are most helpless and who give least promise of making any return; little children whose fathers have died and left them without means, and their mothers, who are all the worse off because they have these little children to provide for. He actually prides Himself on being *their* God. "A father of the fatherless and a judge of the widows is God in His holy habitation" (Ps. 68 : 5).

The ethical principle laid down is that the man who has the most need of you has the greatest claim upon you.

Then we have directions for the manner of beneficence. True religion requires the personal presence of the man where his benevolence is to do good. The tendency of our age is to help others by proxy, through associations for the relief of the poor, orphanages, widows' homes, Sisters of the Stranger, and many other like praiseworthy institutions. There certainly is no harm in working through all these instrumentalities; indeed, they have claims upon us; but no man must content himself with only such working. He must inspect, he must visit, and he must make personal acquaintance with the widow and the fatherless.

(1) This is necessary for his own development. The Captain of our salvation might have remained seated on His throne and have commanded the forces of good to charge against the forces of evil. But He did no such thing. He came down into the thick of the fight, and wore garments rolled in blood, and took scars of human battle on His person to be seen forever in heaven as fadeless marks of His immortal love. The Captain of our salvation became ' perfect through suffering."

(2) It is necessary for those who are helped. How is the widow to feel that you stand to represent the love of her departed husband if she never sees you? How is the orphan to have any idea of fatherhood if he never sees any one who

represents that relation to him? His own father is dead; if you send him only money and clothes and kind words, is that all there is of fatherhood? Remember that children climb to the idea of the Fatherhood of God on their experience of human fatherhood. To a child who never knew its earthly parents the worst of orphanage is that it cuts him off from the human representation of the divine Fatherhood. To such we must strive to apply that gracious lack. It cannot be done without our personal intercourse with the child.

Let it be remembered that the Scriptures do not give a blessing to the man who distributes alms, gives food and clothes and money. This he may do, as Paul points out, without a particle of charity. And it comes to nothing. "Blessed is he that *considereth* the poor" is the Scriptural benediction (Ps. 41 : 1). And the word in this place means the application of the mind so as to make wise conclusions in regard to the matter in hand. It occurs only in Job 24 : 27, Psalm 41 : 1, Psalm 64 : 9, Proverbs 21 : 12, and Daniel 7 : 8, and always with this sense.

Lecky ("History of European Morals," II. 98) well says that "the rich man, prodigal of money, which to him is of little value, but altogether incapable of devoting any personal attention to the object of his alms, often injures society by his donations; but this is rarely the case with that far nobler charity which makes men familiar with the haunts of wretchedness, and follows the object of his care through all the phases of his life."

A LIFE OF PURITY.

Not less necessary than outward beneficence is inward purity. Indeed, that is the spring of all that is good in the outward life, and if not mentioned first, it must be presupposed. And then it would occur to the mind of the writer that there was a danger to purity of character in that very activity of beneficence which he had stated as one of the characteristics of any religion acceptable to God. The phrase "the world" implied to JAMES, as it did to the other early Christians, not *the orderly universe* which the Greek word was originally used to designate, nor its secondary meaning of *human society*, but in a special sense, perhaps it should be called a New Testament sense, *human society in its ungodly bias*. Dean Alford seems to give us its real meaning. "The whole earthly creation, separated from God and lying in sin, which, whether as consisting in the men who serve it, or the enticements which it holds out to evil lust, is to Christians a source of continual defilement." From all the sin that was in the Jewish world, the Hebrew-Christian world, the Roman world, JAMES would have his brethren saved.

Times change. Manners change. Sin puts on different guises and disguises. We cannot be separated from the human society which we are to help. There is as much to soil the soul in the society of the nineteenth century in London and New York as there was in the first century in Rome and Corinth. We must keep ourselves "unspotted from the world" around us, the world which separates itself from God.

So, while not defining religion, JAMES does describe its characteristics, such characteristics as are indispensable for anything that God would call religion, namely, inward purity and outward beneficence.

V.

The Temptation to Partiality.

CHAPTER II., 1-13.

PARTIALITY FOR THE RICH.

HAVING warned his brethren, first, against the temptation to charge their sins to God, and, secondly, against the temptation to fanaticism, JAMES, thirdly, warns them against the temptation to partiality founded on national and inherited prejudice and on the appeals which wealth makes to the imagination.

These are his words in chapter 11 : 1-13: *"My brethren, do not in personal partialities hold the faith of our Lord, the Jesus Christ of Glory. For if there come into your assembly a man be-gold-ringed, in brilliantly-colored clothing, and there come in a poor person in sordid clothing, and you have regard to him wearing the brilliant-colored clothing, and say to him 'Sit thou thus, beautifully,' and say to the poor person 'Stand thou there,' or 'Sit thou thus, by my footstool,' do you not both make distinctions among yourselves and become judges with evil thoughts? Hear, brethren mine, beloved; has not God chosen the poor of the world, who are rich in faith and heirs of that kingdom which He has proclaimed for those who love Him?*

But ye have dishonored the poor. Do not the rich oppress you? Are they not those who drag you to the courts? Are they not those who blaspheme that beautiful name which was called upon you?"

Our author seems to have made himself well acquainted with the different forms of temptation which were likely to assail his beloved Hebrew-Christian brethren scattered abroad among the Gentiles, endeavoring to maintain a spiritual Christianity under the restraints of old inherited prejudices. He had somehow learned that in their church life there had appeared a partiality to persons, which, whether based on national prejudice or social distinctions, was not simply uncharitable, but very unjust, and very destructive of the peace of the Church as well as of the religious life of the individual believer.

His description is very picturesque, whether we fancy the case described as being in the judicial assembly, or in the general congregation for worship, or the Christian community as distinguished from Judaism and paganism. Such conduct was likely to occur, and in any case was detrimental to their Christianity because it was wrong. Whatever is wrong is not only impolitic but unchristian. The parties, rich and poor, may be of those who are differenced only in their estates. It might be a rich Jew and a poor Jew; or a rich Gentile and a poor Gentile but the probability would be that the rich man was the Jew and the poor man the

Gentile, so that here the old and strong national bias would play upon their decisions and their conduct.

The rich man is set before us strikingly. He has splendid dress. It is brilliantly colored, and attracts immediate attention to him. He is not merely elegantly attired; he is gorgeous in his appearance; not only does he wear rings, such and as many as were customary, but he is loaded with rings. In our day, a gentleman may wear his wedding ring or his seal ring, but if we should see a man with four rings on each finger of both hands, we should regard him as over-dressed. If each ring were costly, so that the whole set should represent a fortune, and we knew that the possessor could afford it, we should still regard a man wearing forty rings as a vulgar person. The word which our Common Version renders "with a gold ring" occurs in this place and probably nowhere else, either in New Testament or classic Greek. It has been supposed to have been coined by JAMES, but that is not certain. It has been pointed out (by Bishop Bloomfield) that it is formed analogically, and may be regarded as one of the many thousands of words of the common dialect not preserved in such remains of antiquity as are in our hands. In the rendering "be-gold-ringed," we have endeavored to reproduce the effect of the Greek word the use of which, by JAMES, seems to have been intended to throw contempt upon the "dude" of his time.

GOING TO COURT.

The power of wealth, or the display thereof, over the imagination has always been well known. It had been shown in the first churches of the first century, it is possible, even in their councils for discipline. Two parties have some difficulty. They cannot have recourse to a pagan court—that was not allowed (1 Cor. 6: 1). They take it to the church. But one is rich and the other poor. When they enter, before the trial begins, there is a prejudgment. Some representative person immediately notices the entrance of the party "wearing the gay clothing." It is not simply the texture and cut of the materials; it is the mode in which it is carried on the person. [At first I translated the phrase, "you have recourse to him *flaunting* the brilliantly colored clothing." The word hardly bears so strong a meaning as "flaunt," and yet it does signify something more than mere having one's clothing upon one.] It is that indescribable something brought into the person's carriage by the consciousness of being in richer raiment than those about him.

At the same moment enters his brother, his Christian brother, the other party to the suit. He is poor; poor in spirit, as well as poor in clothes. He is not so well known to his brethren as "the party of the first part." He is a meek man and does not push his way forward.

Let us look in and see what occurs.

Immediately some attentive member of the court obsequiously approaches the brilliant litigant, described by JAMES as the "chrysodactylic party" [a man be-gold-ringed] and brings him to the best chair in the room, and says "Seat yourself; here; that's nice." Then he, or some other person, says to the poor party, "Stand you there." And there is a very great difference between the "here" and the "there," perhaps so great that he who had spoken both words feels some compunction, and mitigates the treatment by informing the poor brother that, if he prefer sitting to standing, he may come and sit down on his footstool! Do not the brother who stands and the brother in the good seat know what the verdict will be? Is there any use of a trial after this? Would not that be disgraceful behavior in a pagan court? How much more in a Christian assembly met for judicial purposes!

GOING TO CHURCH.

But the warning must not be confined to behavior in church courts, if there should be such things. It is still more applicable to assemblies for public worship. Indeed, in the opinion of some, the passage we are considering refers altogether to the congregation assembled for worship.

No one could suspect this most sensible writer of inculcating any sentiment at variance with the duty of giving "honor to whom honor is due."

Office should command respect; wealth is not to be despised; culture is to be desired. The warning is against carrying caste into religious circles, and especially into religious worship. The universal equality of man before man is a Utopian political dream. Men are not born all equal, as among themselves. They are on an equality only before the law and before God.

It is this broad fact, which should be universally acknowledged and acted upon, which makes caste in church such a pernicious thing, especially when that caste is founded on mere distinctions of wealth. If wealth were always the accompaniment of high character, or poverty the unfailing mark of moral unworth, then the man who could afford to be dressed elegantly every day, should be escorted to the highest seat in the synagogue, and the poor man should be content to sit on any footstool. But nothing is more generally known than that there is no connection between the external estate and the inner character. So far is the reality from any such connection that we have all been acquainted with these several cases: (1) that of a really good man who, at one period of his life, was very poor and at another very rich, but always good; (2) that of another man who had had the same change in fortune, and who was always very bad and very mean; (3) that of a man who was good when he was poor and bad when he was rich, and (4) that of a man who was good when he was rich, and bad when he was poor.

In a country like ours, where fortunes are made and lost in a day, how little claim upon our esteem has any man merely for his estate. So often now is that remark made, so often are seen the basest of men and women suddenly blazing in diamonds, that among thoughtful people, the rich, the good rich, the really humble, true, holy, rich people are scarcely secured from the contempt which overlooks their worth in despising their wealth. This is a mistake on the other side. But it is not so often made as that to which JAMES calls the attention of his brethren.

The lesson to us, in our age, is to exclude caste from churches, in public worship if not elsewhere. Whatever makes a poor man or poor woman feel unwelcome in a church is a wrong against Christian charity. If it be in the church building, or in the behavior of the ushers or in the arrangement of the pews, or in the dress of the worshippers, it is the very thing against which the principle set forth by JAMES is levelled. If there be any seats better than other seats they should be open equally to all in turn; if there be inferior seats they should be voluntarily occupied by all in turn. If ushers are to make any difference in escorting worshippers to seats that difference should be made in favor of those who have the poorest appearance, or are known to be poor—not because they are poor, but because they are apt to be more sensitive, knowing the deference which mere worldlings show to mere wealth.

Perhaps, in the modern church worship, the greatest discouragement which the poor feel, is in the dress which their rich brethren and sisters are accustomed to exhibit in the house of God. It is a shame to their poor apparel. It ought to be a shame to any well-to-do Christian woman when she wears her gayest and newest costly clothing to public worship, and appears with diamonds and other very valuable and conspicuous ornaments before the altars of her God. Cannot the Christian women of this age at length have courage to refuse to continue to be Sunday advertisements of modistes and milliners? A lady in New York, whose pew was on one of the wall sides of the church, and who consequently had the congregation all on one side of her, suggested to her milliner that she put a certain bow on the "congregation side" of her bonnet! What a revelation was that! And was it solitary? Is not the preparation of many a worshipper made *on the congregation side?* And is not the House of the Lord thus turned into a show-room, in which those who have no special dry-goods to exhibit are neither welcome nor at home?

EVIL OF PARTIALITY.

See the evil of this partiality. In those who indulge it, it works a confusion of intellectual ideas and moral sentiments. It blunts their judgment. They form decisions on wrong grounds. They do injustice to others. They make unneeded and hurtful distinctions between brethren. They create schisms in the body of Christ. No good is done, and much evil.

ON THE SIDE OF THE POOR.

The unreasonableness and injustice of this are next shown. With a tender, imploring tone, JAMES solicits the attention of his readers. "Hear, brethren mine."

(1) Then he points out to them that those Christians whom they had despised were the favorites of heaven. If God is wise in His choice, are you not foolish in your discrimination? When He has made choice of men for any special and grand work in the Church, He has ordinarily chosen those who were poor, as the world ranks poverty. They had neither much land nor much money. They neither had great civil rank or high social position. The men that have sung the songs which are to be the solace of the sorrowful and the stimulant of the faithful, have been taken from such low places as that from which David ascended to the throne. The men who were to propagate a fresh faith by preaching a new evangel, have been the men like those whom the Son of God found washing fishermen's nets on a little lake in an obscure corner of the planet. The men who have reformed an apostate Church, have been men who were born in the hut of the poor miner, like Martin Luther. When the Son of God, Himself the Lord of glory, comes to wear

human flesh, and so make a perpetual alliance with our humanity, He does not honor the daughter of a king or Crœsus by becoming her babe, but condescends to be born of a virgin who has no special distinction, no high place, and no material possessions. And among His followers, down to the day of JAMES, down to our day, not so many rich have been the servants of the Lord; the poor have always been very greatly in the majority. As one has said, "God has more rent and better paid Him from a smoky cottage than from many stately palaces, where men wallow in wealth, and forget God." Surely, God's favorites generally are not rich.

(2) It is to be noticed that there are different kinds of riches. What is wealth? Is it always money? What is the worth of money beyond its purchasing power? A dollar or a pound can purchase more at one time than at another, in one place than in another. If I have thousands of dollars or of pounds in the middle of the desert, where I am separated from all men, I cannot purchase therewith an ounce of bread or meat, a gill of coffee or water. JAMES knew the purchasing power of stamped coin, but he also knew that other things have procuring value. Toward the seen "world" money makes a man rich; but it has no power whatever toward the unseen world. There "faith" is the legal tender. A man may be penniless toward the world, yet able to procure all

the things needful for his spirit, so that he may become wise, and great, and true, and heroic, and lofty, and happy. Among those who are "the poor of the world" are multitudes who are among the millionaires of faith, being the chosen of God. And God's measure of a man, and every wise man's measure of his fellow, is not according to his height, or weight, or age, or social position, or money, or intellect, or learning; it is according to his *faith*, to his power of perceiving, receiving, and retaining truth (Romans 12: 3). A man may not be very rich in the possession of much faith, but *any* faith is riches, and the more faith the more wealth. And often, how great is the faith of the otherwise poor.

(3) Not only are many who are of "the poor of the world" chosen of God and rich in faith, but they are also heirs to future greatness. Hebrew-Christians were still proud of their blood; they were not of the "Gentiles," the "nations" ruled by fools or knaves; they were of the theocracy, the kingdom whose king was Jehovah. Now, JAMES reminds his old friends and parishioners, that those Gentiles who had become their brethren in Christ, although they were still the poor of the world, were favorites of God, being at present rich with a riches which does not vouch for itself by the display of gold rings and brilliant raiment; but also that they are heirs [non-apparent, indeed, but] real heirs of a kingdom made good to them by

the promises of that God who to Abraham had conveyed by similar promises the covenant which had secured to his children all those things which they had so richly enjoyed and of which they were so justly proud.

Yes, my beloved brethren, JAMES would say; they are brothers of yours; brothers adopted into the family of Abraham's God through the Christ-Son of that God; and they are that God's favorites; and, although they have not that which can be used as legal tender in the world's financial transactions, they have a currency good in all the streets of the city of God; a currency which provides for them that which is far above all lands and houses, and sumptuous appointments, and brilliant equipages; and they are hereafter to sit on thrones and judge the world (1 Cor. 6: 2); and judge angels (1 Cor. 6: 3), and some of them shall judge the twelve tribes of Israel (Matt. 19: 28). And these you have "despised," because they were "poor." You have done them injustice at your ecclesiastical tribunals, and dishonor in your assemblies for public worship. Oh, my beloved brethren!

ON THE SIDE OF THE RICH.

Then he calls their attention to the characteristics of those very rich persons, to gain whose favor they had sacrificed justice and charity. "They had money." Well, what effect had that money had upon their characters, and how had it been employed by them? As a rule, in all ages of the world, great riches have had a tendency to make men selfish, arrogant, and oppressive. What has not been spent on pampering themselves, the rich had usually employed to oppress the poor. Those to whom JAMES wrote probably knew instances in which the rich Jews and rich pagans had "lorded it imperiously" over poor Christians, drawing them into pagan courts, and using the power of their money to bring undeserved sufferings on the saints.

But there was something worse than that, which, at least, should seem worse to every true Christian heart. Those rich men had blasphemed that beautiful and reverent name by which Christians had been called in baptism. Of course, those who persecuted Christians as Christians, would spit upon the name by which they were called; but there were others also, who had not put themselves to the trouble of persecuting, but who had blasphemed that fair name. And these, JAMES would seem to say, are they for whose worthless favor you have put aside the claims of those who were saints, because those saints were not rich!

A REPLY TO THE DEFENCE OF THE PARTIALIST.

"If in truth you fulfil that royal law 'Love thou thy neighbor as thyself,' you do beautifully. But if you show personal partiality, you work sin, being convicted by the law as transgressors. For whoso-

ever shall keep the whole law and yet fall in one, he has become arrested of all. For He that said 'Thou shalt not commit adultery,' said also 'Thou shalt not steal.' Now, if thou dost not commit adultery, but dost steal, thou hast become a transgressor of the law. So speak and so act as those who are about to be judged through a law of liberty. For merciless judgment is to him who does not act mercy; mercy glorieth against judgment" (8-13).

To see the connection of this statement with what went before, it is to be remembered that JAMES is addressing those who were Jews by birth, or under the influence of Judaizing teachers. To the strong things he had said he may have supposed some one to be replying, that in his attention to rich but unworthy people, he was simply obeying the law which commands each man to love his neighbor as himself! If that was so, it would be very much like that of which so many men in our age are guilty, the employment of Scripture for the defence of wrong. It has been said sometimes sneeringly that something can be found in the Bible for everything and every occasion. What a compliment to the fulness of the Bible. Yes, even the devil finds in Holy Scripture some baits for the hooks he throws out in fishing. When he came tempting Jesus, he employed inspired language. But how different are Bible phrases and Bible truth when quoted by Satan and by Jesus!

To meet the disingenuous defence JAMES does not belittle the law. On the contrary, he maintains it, and dignifies it by calling it "the royal law." And so it is. The law of love is royal. It stands king among the commands, and makes all the others great; it ennobles all who live in the air of its blessed spirit; and it crowns life with beauty and glory. But the law must be revered and obeyed in its entirety, and should govern the Christian quite as much in his treatment of the poor as in his treatment of the rich. "Respect of persons" for circumstances rather than for their character is sinful. The Hebrew-Christians should have remembered Deut. 16 : 19, 20, " Thou **shalt** not wrest judgment; thou shalt not respect persons; that which is altogether just shalt thou follow." They were convicted as sinful by the very law which they professed to keep.

It is a disgrace to one's intellect to quote the law in justification of one's behavior in one thing, when the authority of that law is thrown aside entirely in another. It is not good to behave in this way. But it is beautiful to have the hand of that law laid evenly on the whole of a man's life.

A GREAT PRINCIPLE.

And that leads our writer to lay down the great general principle, that whosoever shall keep the whole law and yet fail in one as certainly lays himself open to punishment as the man who has no regard for any portion of the commands. Undoubtedly the case is of so frequent occurrence in our day that every reader of these pages must know scores of people who are described by this passage, people who claim to be moral, who suppose themselves to be moral, who acknowledge the demands of the law and seem to yield it a kind of general obedience, and yet keep some one command which they deliberately and habitually violate in public or in private. In JAMES'S day, the Rabbins taught that if a man kept a single one of the commandments faultlessly he would remain in the favor of God. This teaching found such acceptance with them that it was usual, in practice, to select one precept for careful observance, generally the law of the Sabbath, the law of sacrifice, or the law of tithes, looking upon these as the greater commands, making little account of mercy and judgment, which were so much in the eyes of Jesus. Against this most demoralizing teaching JAMES lays the exalted and uplifting doctrine of *the inviolability of the whole law*.

We do well to confirm ourselves in the truth of this great principle. Let us consider three things.

1. It is not merely the violation of God's law we are to regard, but the temper which leads thereto. Sinfulness is to the sinner a greater evil than the sin. The sin is something outside of himself; the sinfulness inside. He has projected the sin out of himself, to be a black fact in

God's universe; the sinfulness remains in him to be the black parent of other sinful acts. If all his past sins were suddenly annihilated and still his sinfulness remained he would be a sinner. It is the case of a rebel whose king may have forgiven him, but who still nourishes the rebellious spirit in his heart. One single sin, presumptuously and habitually indulged, proves the existence of the spirit of rebellion to divine authority. The sovereign cannot tolerate any subject who holds himself free from any single law of the realm. There may be an external obedience without loyalty, for loyalty implies love. He is not a patriot who serves his country, or keeps his country's laws, for fear of loss, or hope of reward. He is not a true child who keeps his father's commands to the letter while he hates the command and dislikes the father. The religion of Jesus is in the heart. If a man has obeyed the Heavenly Father through fear, Jesus desires to bring him to such a state of heart that his love for the Father will make obedience to the Father's commands spontaneous and delightful. If any one law be sequestrated, kept apart for violation, the child is as certainly disloyal, the man is as certainly a sinner, as if the whole law were set at defiance.

2. JAMES urges the fact that each law has been enacted by the authority which makes every other law obligatory. This unity of authority was set forth in the law, as quoted by Jesus

(Mark 12 : 29), "The Lord our God, the Lord is one," and responded to by the scribe with whom He was conversing : " Of a verity, Teacher, thou hast well said that He is one ; and there is none other but He." It is not difficult, then, to perceive that all the commandments are included in each single commandment, the violation of which will put the violator under arrest. And it may be well to note, that this great principle sets every law enacted by our Heavenly Father in the light of sacredness, so that it seems a solecism to speak of any sins as " little sins," and any lies as " white lies." Much less would little sins be excusable, if there were little sins. They require less resistance, while, like the little speck on the skin of the fruit, they may eat in and destroy all.

3. There is no middle ground between this principle and the surrender of all government. If a thing is permissible, a wise Ruler should not forbid it. If a thing is hurtful, a wise Father should not allow it. If, in all the whole category of laws, any one may be set aside, or the violation of any be indulged with impunity, then either God must select the law from which the divine sanction is to be lifted, or the man who desires to sin must make the selection.

If God be supposed to select, we have the extraordinary suggestion of the Father cherishing disobedience in the child, the monarch affording aid to the rebel, the only perfectly holy person in the universe sanctioning sin.

But if each man is to select his pet sin to be indulged with impunity, he must do this either with or without the approbation of God. It cannot be the former, as that would be a case of God sanctioning sin, which cannot be entertained for a moment. And how are we to conceive of a man selecting a single sin for his indulgence without the permission of God? But, suppose we could take in that idea; then the following would result. Each man would reason from the liberty of the others to a larger liberty for himself, and so the area of rebellion would be perpetually enlarging. If all selected the same sin the terrific state of society may be imagined. Suppose, for instance, all men kept every other commandment, but all felt at liberty to violate the eighth in the Decalogue. The absolute worthlessness of all property would immedietely ensue, and the progress of civilization come to a dead halt. Suppose all carefully obeyed every precept of the law but the sixth, and every man felt at liberty to commit homicide at any time. It is plain that all the wit and energy of each man would be concentrated on the preservation of a life which would be worthless, because it would be reduced to a mere existence, denied of every pleasure which comes from human intercourse. In this case, as well as in the case of one man selecting lying, and another adultery, and another theft, and another murder, it is plain that human society would dissolve and the moral government of the universe would collapse.

A NECESSARY PRINCIPLE.

This is so plainly a necessary principle of all government that it is acknowledged in all known codes of human jurisprudence. That a man has paid every debt but one would not discharge the obligation to pay *that* debt. Many a man has been hanged for a solitary act of malicious homicide. To the defence of the accused might be brought proof of a general course of even exemplary conduct. No suspicion had ever been expressed of violation by him of any other law than the law against murder, and it might be urged that not only had the accused never been suspected of any other murder, but that no one had ever known him to express anything but charitable and even generous sentiments. Still, while there remained the undeniable and overwhelming proof of the killing of one man with malice aforethought, thus fixing the guilt of murder upon him, although he had kept the whole law, having failed, fallen, offended the law, in one instance, "he has become arrested of all." A man that has been hanged for a single murder has suffered as much as could be inflicted upon him if he had violated a thousand times every principle of constitutional law, and every enactment of statute law.

A GUARDED EXPRESSION.

Now, let us mark that this uncommonly sensible pastor does not teach his scattered parishioners that a man who has committed one sin is as *guilty* as if he had committed a thousand; nor that a man who has violated one commandment is as bad a man as if he had daily set the whole decalogue at defiance and shaped his life to throw contempt on the whole body of divine law. Neither must he be supposed to teach that there is but one grade of criminality, which is reached by every sinner in his first sin, nor that all violations of God's law are of equal heinousness. But he does teach that one sin, any one sin, is as *certainly* a violation of God's law, representing God's authority and majesty, as would be any form of casting off the soul's allegiance to God.

What is still more, the man who has done this, who has sequestrated to himself some department of morals in which he has regarded himself as free from the authority of God, so that he has committed some certain sin habitually, as if it were a permissible indulgence, is not the man who can claim to be saved *by the law;* and this is precisely the case JAMES had in hand. The persons whose conduct he was arraigning, justified themselves by an appeal to the law, whose authority they had thrown off. It was as if a murderer should plead for discharge on the ground that he had never stolen. His argument would be that the strict observance of the eighth commandment set him free to disregard the sixth.

JAMES shows his readers what Paul showed his, namely, that by the deeds of the law no man can be shown to be just, since all men have stumbled at some point, and so are under arrest for violation of law. We cannot be saved if we reject the mercy of God, and insist upon resting our case on perfect obedience to a perfect law. When a man rejects the mercy of God, he must abide by the legal judgment of God.

But the persons to whom JAMES wrote had accepted God's mercy in Jesus Christ. To a believer the law is not grievous; it is his life. To one out of Christ the law is a bondage, a restraint. He does good, he ever does right, by a constraint from without. He is drawn to duty by the law, as if a man were pulled along the right road by ropes wherewith he had been bound. The true believer is impelled to doing right and doing good from an inner impulse, an impulse of love for God created by the mercy of God. It is a law to him, but it is a law of love, and JAMES says it is a law of liberty. His service is perfect freedom whom we love to obey.

CHOOSE MERCY.

What shall we choose? Let us choose mercy. We cannot abide the judgment of God in its strictness, if we solicit a verdict for our lives by the demands of the law. Let us throw ourselves on God's mercy. Awfully holy as is the judgment of God, the mercy of God is more awfully beautiful and glorious. It triumphs over judgment, as a superior over an inferior. The Heavenly Father glories in it more than in judgment.

The practical moral effect upon our conduct should be to lead us to be more than just and impartial, not only doing right by all men, but as we have opportunity doing "good unto all men, especially to them that are of the household of faith." And we must never forget that as mercy is the quality of His nature which is most delightful to God, that quality in Himself in which He most glories, so mercilessness in man is the thing which our Lord will least tolerate, because it is the thing He most abhors.

VI.

Faith and Works.

CHAPTER II: 14–26.

JUSTIFICATION.

JAMES proceeds to inculcate holy and charitable living, as important to assure a believer that he *is* a believer, and to justify his faith to the world by proving (1) that he really holds the faith which he professes and (2) that that faith is a living and fruitful power in his spirit.

That we may have before us the whole statement, let us read critically the entire passage from the fourteenth verse to the end of the second chapter.

"*What profit is it, brothers mine, if one claim to have faith, but have not works? If a brother or sister become naked and lacking daily food, and one among you say to them, 'Go in peace, be warmed and fattened,' while ye do not give to them the things needful for the body,—what profit is it? Thus also that faith, seeing it has not works, is dead, being by itself. But says one 'Thou hast faith and I have works. Show me that faith of thine by thy works, and I will show thee by my works that faith of mine. Thou believest that*

God is one? Well doest thou; even the demons believe, and shudder.' But art thou willing to know, O empty man, that the faith without works is dead? Abraham, the father of us—was he not by works made just, in offering his son Isaac upon the altar? Thou seest that faith was co-operating with his works, and by works the faith made complete; and the Scripture was fulfilled, which said 'Abraham put his faith in God and it was counted to him for righteousness [uprightness] and he was called God's-friend.' You see then that by works a man is made upright [righteous] and not by faith only. And likewise also was not Rahab the harlot made just by works, receiving the messengers and sending them out another way? For as the body without the spirit is dead, so also faith without works is dead."

We come now to a much-discussed part of the Epistle of JAMES, upon which great strength has been needlessly wasted and many profitless words have been spoken and written. May we be saved from adding thereto!

JAMES AND PAUL.

In the first place, there has been the sinister criticism that the words of JAMES antagonize those of Paul, and, in the second place, that they were intended to correct the teachings of the Apostle. The groundlessness of all this appears (1) from the fact that a careful examination of the paths travelled by the two writers, beginning at different stations, come together in the end; that is, that while treating two different subjects, in fundamentals they agree; (2) that this epistle can not be regarded as a criticism upon the Epistle to the Romans, seeing that Paul's letter is supposed to have been published after the Epistle of JAMES, and that there is no historic evidence that JAMES ever saw or heard of the Epistle to the Romans during his whole life; and (3) those who believe that both writers wrote as they were moved by the Holy Ghost, know that there must be agreement in all essentials, and that any appearance of disagreement, if there be such, must be due to the defective intelligence of the reader.

Let us notice the classes of persons severally addressed by these writers. They are not all of one class. When Paul is writing in regard to justification by faith, he is considering the class of unregenerate men, men who neither have nor claim perfect uprightness but are supposed to be sincerely and anxiously asking the question, how a man is to be justified with God. JAMES is considering the class of men who are regenerate, or suppose themselves so, who believe that they have been justified as to God and must now establish their claim to righteousness with their fellow-men.

He had already in the former chapter shown that he held what is called the doctrine of " justification by faith," only he had chosen to express it, or perhaps it were better to say that he naturally expressed it, in the language of his brother Jesus, in phraseology common to two men who had grown up in the same family. He had said that our regeneration had its source in God, the Giver of good gifts (as Jesus had said (Matt. 7: 11) "How much more shall your Father in heaven give good things to them that ask Him!) and that the instrument was "the word of God" (as Jesus had said (John 17: 17) when praying to the Father, "Sanctify them through Thy truth, Thy word is truth") and that the condition was our faith; "receive with meekness the ingrafted word which is able to save your souls," (as Jesus had said "that whosoever believed in Him may have endless life" (John 3: 15), and (John 6: 47), "He that believeth on Me hath endless life").

The comparison of the deliverances of these two inspired men of God shows that if the doctrine of "justification by faith" is set forth by Paul logically, the same doctrine is set forth by JAMES more evangelically; that is, less in the language of the schools and more in the language attributed by the Evangelists to Jesus; the one addressing the logical understanding of the unregenerate man, the other appealing to the heart of the professed Christian.

THEOLOGY AND ETHICS.

It may be profitable to see how the great theological teacher agrees with the great ethical teacher. It would be doing injustice to Paul to suppose, as many do, that he taught that nothing was necessary beyond a mere intellectual assent to the doctrines of Christianity, that he thus yielded to the ruinous teaching of some of the Jewish rabbis and the disastrous belief of the great mass of the Jews of his own day, namely, that assent to the truth is all that is requisite for salvation, thus inculcating that faith which JAMES demonstrates to be "dead." Paul's "faith" is represented in the vivacious language of Luther: "Oh, faith is a lively, busy, active thing, so that it is impossible for it not to be ceaselessly working good; it does not ask if good works are to be done, but before it asks it has done them, and is ever doing."

So Paul says things like these: "If I had all faith, so as to remove mountains, and have not love, I am nothing" (1 Cor. 13:2). And "Now abide, faith, hope, love; and the greatest of these is love" (1 Cor. 13:13). And "Stand fast in the faith; quit you like men; be strong; let all that ye do be done in love" (1 Cor. 16:13). And "Faith *worketh* by love" (Gal. 5:6), which is simply another way of putting JAMES'S teaching on this subject. A faith that does not work is no faith, and a faith that works, but does not work by love is a profitless faith. It is now quite plain that when Paul is teaching that in order to stand uprightly before God one must have faith, and puts it thus (Rom. 3:28): "We reckon that a man is made just by faith apart from the works of law," he is teaching that a man is regenerated not by what he does in striving to avoid a violation of the law, but by his faith in God's words. And we must not fail to notice, that what Paul calls "the works of the law" are very different from the works of which JAMES is writing. The former were the things done by an unregenerate man, from obedience to the law and for the profit of the doer, who expected thereby to be justified; the latter, the things done by a regenerate man from love, for the benefit of others.

JAMES plainly believed that there was no faith which does not produce such good works as these. If a man supposed himself to be justified by his faith, how is his faith to be justified? How is he to be sure he has the faith that makes him just before God? It is by the works of love produced by that faith. That faith will surely produce those works. It could not exist without working, so if no works of love appear, it is manifest that no living faith exists.

This is seen in the opening words of his address on this subject. He is not speaking of a man who really has faith, but of a man who claims to have the faith he does not possess. He states and examines only *the claim*. As his brother Jesus had put the question as to what *profit* there is gaining the world if the soul be lost, and Paul had put the question as to what *profit* there is in works which might help others but were devoid of the grace of charity, so JAMES put the question as to what *profit* there is in making a claim when the claimant can point to nothing whatever that can be helpful in substantiating that claim. What profit, what help, to him who makes it or to others, is a claim that something is a living thing, when it never presents any of the phenomena of life, never sees, hears, feels, speaks, or moves?

It is to be kept in mind that JAMES is not speaking of the faith that justifies, that is, that makes a man just before God, apart from those works of the law which the man does (which is the faith Paul speaks of in Rom. 3:28,) nor of faith in general. He does not ask, "Can faith save him?" But he does ask, "Can *that* faith save him?" What faith? A worthless, inoperative faith. There is often a strong assertion in a question. Indeed, sometimes it is the most forcible way of making an assertion. JAMES plainly intended that the question should have the force of a very emphatic assertion. If Paul had ever read this question in the Epistle of James, his answer would probably have been an emphatic declaration: "No, such a faith as that could save no man; neither can any other faith than that faith which worketh through love, as I said in my epistle to the Galatians" (Gal. 5:6). There is no value in any faith, or any charity, or any work which does not "save," which does not preserve a man's character.

You believe in God the Father Almighty; do you? You believe in Jesus Christ His Son, who tasted death for every man; do you? You believe in the sentence which was so often on the lips of Jesus Christ, "It is more blessed to give than to receive"; do you? We shall see whether that faith exist or whether only your claim to it exist, whether you possess the faith, that faith that works by love, or are merely an empty professor.

Such may be supposed to be the address of JAMES to the professor of that faith in Jesus which justifies a man, which saves a man, which makes a man fit to live and fit to die.

THE PRACTICAL TEST.

Then our writer paints a picture. The claimant to saving faith has means. He is not a pauper. Two persons are known to him, a man and a woman. A woman in want is a very sad sight; perhaps a man in want is sadder. When a man cannot support himself by reason of any providential hindrance, we know that whatever manhood is in him must suffer intensely. He says to himself, "A woman cannot be expected to support herself, but I'm a man; and it's disgraceful for a man to be dependent for his subsistence upon another." This professor of faith finds *a man*, a real true man, not a heathen, not an infidel, not a blasphemer, not an impostor, but a good, true man, a brother in Christ, who is no tramp, who has never begged, who does not even beg from the professor, who has toiled with his own hands, providing things that are honest in the sight of God; but now he is down in the world. He has no longer strength to do enough work each day to gain that day's bread. And his clothing is insufficient. It has been washed and patched until it has become too worn to keep him comfortable, and too shabby to allow him to go into decent society. And the "professor" says, "Brother, go in peace," and shows him out. The "go" is plainly from the heart, and the "in peace" is manifestly cant. And next day, the professor says that same to a woman, who is a woman of good fame and faith, being the professor's "sister," that is if the blood of Jesus runs in him. But she is deeply reduced. "Go in peace. Be warmed. Be fattened," says the claimant to saving faith. But the "brother" gets no food from him, and the "sister" goes off shivering in her thin garments. Neither the brother nor the sister carries away anything which will make life more tolerable.

Next day, JAMES is supposed to have met the "professor of religion" with whom he has had argument, and catechizes him on the result of yesterday's interview. "You had faith, had you? Well, what profit was it? It did you no good. It did not save you from being a mean, heartless, unbrotherly man. It did not profit the brother, nor did it profit the sister. It did not satisfy their hunger, nor protect them from the cold. It was helpful neither inwardly nor outwardly. Your faith is dead. If it were not, it would give proof of life ; but it is as much alive as a bulb buried in a stone tomb, which, being separated from earth, and light, and the fresh air, is soon a dead thing, if ever it were alive."

FACTS OF EXPERIENCE.

Here our writer points to most important facts in human experience, namely, (1) that that which ceases to grow begins to decay, and (2) that a continuance of life without exercise is impracticable. Let the case be supposed of a man suddenly endowed with the liveliest conceivable faith. If that faith is not exercised it dies. No man can long believe in God the Father Almighty who goes weeks and months behaving as if he and all the universe were orphaned. No man can long believe that Jesus Christ is his Savior who does not allow Jesus Christ to save him. No man can long believe in the brotherhood of man who never treats any other man as if he were his brother. In this it appears that faith without works is dead.

But this pertinacious, do-nothing professor of religion is met by a sincere Christian, who says to him, "Thou hast faith and I have works." The suggestion seems to be that, for a moment and for the argument, we may admit that faith and good works may exist apart. Then, how is the inoperative faith to prove its existence? How is it possible to demonstrate the existence of life in the absence of vital phenomena? "Prove your faith," says the true Christian. "You know that there is no other way than by good works; but you admit that you have no good works, nay, that you even scorn them; you cannot, therefore, show your faith." A true Christian faith always produces good works and thus has its credentials. A man's faith is invisible; so is the vegetable vitality in the sap of an apple-tree. How are we to know that the sap is in the tree and is alive, if no fruit nor even blossoms come?

The true Christian interlocutor goes on to tighten the grip on the conscience of the man who professes to have a faith which he acknowledges to be inoperative. He argues thus: "You believe that faith, and faith alone, the mere intellectual assent of the mind to the truth, will save a man. Well, let us try it. The fundamental truth of religion is that indispensable truth without which no religion, true or false, can exist, namely, *there is a God*. Of any true religion the basal truth is *God is one*. You believe that. It is well. But does faith in that immense truth save? Your proposition is, that if any one believe any great religious truth he is saved. But the demons, who are as orthodox as the archangel on the fundamental doctrine of religion, are not saved. Then one may believe and not be saved. The faith of the demons produces no good works, but many evil works. They believe and shudder ; they do not rejoice in believing. They believe ; they were prompt to assert their belief in the Son of God when He was upon earth. Were any of them saved ? No; they were all cast out. The most conspicuous example in the universe of a firmly fixed faith in the foundation truth of religion, is to be seen in the most thoroughly unsaved persons in the universe—the lost demons; they who have a dead faith, are themselves as dead as the demons."

THE CASE OF ABRAHAM.

Then, either JAMES or the Christian who is supposed to be laboring with the self-deceived "professor of religion," who was a Hebrew-Christian, presses him still further. He is addressed as an empty man, in whose hands are neither seed for sowing nor gathered sheaves. In such a condition, he is asked whether he is willing to know that his inoperative faith is dead ? The hearer was a descendant of Abraham, who is at the other pole from the demons. Abraham was "justified"; no one questions that. Why does no one question that ? For the following reasons : He was called out of Ur of the Chaldees, and he believed that he should go (Gen. 12). How did he know, and how were others to know, that he believed that he should go from his country, and his kindred, and his father's house, after God had promised to make him a great nation, and in him to bless all the families of the earth? Because he "*departed*, as the Lord had said unto him." He might have staid in Ur of the Chaldees for a century, professing to have faith in God; but neither man nor God would have discovered it. But the long and tiresome journey from Haran in Mesopotamia, to Sichem, near the Mediterranean Sea, under the depressing influence of exile from his native place, a bereavement of which scarcely any man in Christendom has the least conception in this century, in which almost every man dies where he was not born—that journey justified him.

That faith which works grows stronger after this exhibition of his faith. The Lord made a fresh covenant with him to give him and his children the land in which he was. And the years went by, and there was no child born to Abraham; but while he brooded over the promise to his seed, the promise that he should become a great nation, there was no sign of the coming first child. And still his estate grew richer, and he fought his battles out to victory, his faith clinging to the promise of a great family, while yet there was no child. And the years went, and Abraham was ninety and nine years old, and God's promise was repeated, and yet no child came. But as he closed his century the child came. Isaac was born.

But who was to know that Abraham had been faithful all this time? And as Isaac grew, who was to know that he was a man justified by faith? God knew that faith without works, if it were not dead, would die; and without works would remain forever incomplete. And so the divinely appointed test came. And Abraham's faith co-operated with his works; and the offering of his Isaac completed his faith. So the Scripture was fulfilled which said (Gen. 15 : 6), "He believed the Lord and it was counted to him for righteousness." Why was it so "counted?" Because it *was* righteousness. Faith in God is righteousness, and makes a man righteous. Men often impute to a man that which he really has not. The Lord can never make any such mistake. When he accounts that a man has anything, the man has that thing. JAMES believed that a man is justified by faith, but, as he says, not "by faith only." Paul believed that a man is justified by works, but not "by works only," for whatsoever is not of faith is sin (Romans 14 : 23). It is to be noticed that the same passage, from Gen. 15 : 6, is employed by the Apostle Paul (Romans 4 : 4), in his argument on justification by faith.

THE PHILOTHEANS.

Not only did God count Abraham's faith for righteousness, but after his offering of Isaac, men had such respect for Abraham that they called him "God's-friend," a Philothean. Mark, he is not called "*the* friend of God" so as to separate him from all men of faith, but the name given him assigns him to a class of persons into which they come, and only they, whose faith in God is exhibited to the world by works of love toward their fellow-men; they are all Philotheans, none other can justly be called by that excellent name. It began with Abraham. It was reinstituted by Jesus the Lord (John 15 : 8): "Herein is My Father glorified, that ye bear much fruit; and *so* shall ye be My disciples. Even as the Father hath loved Me, I also have loved you: abide ye in My love. If ye keep My commandments, ye shall abide in My love; even as I have kept My Father's commandments, and abide in His love. These things have I spoken unto you, that My joy may be in you, and that your joy may be fulfilled. This is My commandment, that ye love one another, even as I have loved you. Greater love hath no man than this, that a man lay down his life for his *friends*. Ye are *My friends*, if ye do the things which I command you. No longer do I call you slaves; for the slave knoweth not what his lord doeth: but I have called you *friends;* for all things that I heard from My Father I have made known unto you. Ye did not choose Me, but I chose you, and appointed you, that ye should go and bear fruit, and that your fruit should abide."

THE CASE OF RAHAB.

JAMES had selected the most splendid instance among men, and that which above every human name would attract the attention and command the respect of those to whom he wrote. That his argument might be complete, he now cites the case of a Gentile, who was a woman, who was a harlot. To her there had come an account of Jehovah's terrible things in Egypt and stupendous doings in the desert, and what He had done to the two kings of the Amorites, that were on the other side of Jordan, Sihon and Og, whom He had utterly destroyed. Knowing His power and His promise, she believed Him. Before she had seen one of the people to whom she believed that Jehovah had given her land, she had lived in secret faith. If she had had opportunity to display that faith in works of goodness and had not done so, her faith would have died. No one knew it. But when the time came in which she could show her faith by her works, she received and delivered the spies of Joshua as the messenger of the true God, she made a profession of her faith, she abandoned her former sinful life, attached herself to the people of God, and spent the rest of her life in the service of Jehovah. Of what use would her faith have been if unaccompanied by good works? Would she have been saved? On the contrary, she would have been lost, and the whole force of her life would have been with her. A dead faith cannot quicken a spirit into holy living. But her works, which sprang from faith, justified her faith. In her ignorance of the high demand for veracity made by her new religion, she had lied; but her faith worked by love and purified her heart, and she was admitted into the glorious company of the Philotheans, and died in the midst of Israel, a true daughter of Abraham.

FREDERICK W. ROBERTSON'S ILLUSTRATION.

After all, do sincere and simple hearts make any trouble out of the apparent contradiction? Is it not cynical, sinister, bent souls, or men who delight to put off their duty on any plea, even the slightest, who are glad to find what can be raised in an excuse for wrong-doing? Voltaire could find something to sneer at in the seeming opposition of Paul and JAMES, but not such a clear-headed, lofty-spirited man as Frederick W. Robertson. The latter says, "Suppose I say, 'A tree cannot be struck without thunder;' that is true, for there is never destructive lightning without thunder. But again, if I say, 'The tree was struck by lightning without thunder,' that is true too, if I mean that the lightning alone struck it without the thunder striking it. Yet read the two assertions together, and they seem contradictory. So, in the same way, Paul says, 'Faith justifies without works,'—that is, faith alone is that which justifies us, not works. But JAMES says, 'Not a faith which is without works.' There will be works with faith, as there is thunder with lightning; but just as it is not the thunder, but the lightning, the lightning without the thunder, that strikes the tree, so it is not the works which justify. Put it in one sentence—*faith alone* justifies, but not the *faith which is alone*. Lightning alone strikes, but not the lightning which is alone, without thunder; for that is only summer lightning, and harmless."

ARCHBISHOP WHATELY'S ILLUSTRATION.

Practical life sweeps away the cobwebs of sophistry. Archbishop Whately tells the following instructive story. Two gentlemen were one day crossing the river in a ferry-boat. A dispute about faith and works arose, one saying that good works were of small importance, and that faith was everything, the other asserting the contrary. Not being able to convince each other, the ferryman, an enlightened Christian, asked permission to give his opinion. Consent being granted, he said: "I hold in my hands two oars. That in my right hand I call 'faith,' the other, in my left, 'works.' Now, gentlemen, please to observe, I pull the oar of faith, and pull that alone. See! the boat goes round and round, and the boat makes no progress. I do the same with the oar of works, and with a precisely similar result—no advance. Mark! I pull both together, we go on apace, and in a very few minutes we shall be at our landing-place. So, in my humble opinion," he added, "faith without works, or works without faith, will not suffice. Let there be both, and the haven of eternal rest is sure to be reached."

VII.

Temptations of the Tongue.

CHAPTER III., 1–18.

FANATICISM AND THE TONGUE.

THE fourth form of temptation is presented in the third chapter: *"Do not become many of you teachers, brethren mine, since ye know that we shall receive heavier judgment. For, in many things we all stumble. If any one stumble not in word, the same is a perfect man, and able also to bridle the whole body. Behold into their mouths we put the horse-bits, that they may become obedient unto us, and we turn about their whole body. Behold also the ships, which though they may be so great and are driven by rough winds, are turned about by a very small rudder, whither the impulse of the steersman may will; so the tongue also is a little member, and boasts greatly. Behold how a spark kindles a great forest. And the tongue is fire; that world of iniquity! Thus the tongue is placed among our members, which stains the whole body and sets on fire the frame of nature and is set on fire of hell. For every nature of wild beasts, and of flying things and of creeping things, and of sea-monsters is subdued and has been subdued unto human nature;*

but the tongue of men no one can subdue—a turbulent evil, full of death-bearing poison; with it we praise God, even the Father, and with it we curse men made in the image of God: from the same mouth come forth a eulogy and a curse. No necessity, my brethren, that these things sho.ld be so. Does a fountain from the same opening send forth sweet and bitter? My brethren, can a fig tree produce olives, or a vine figs? So cannot salt water yield sweet."

In urging the necessity of a faith which gives demonstrations of its existence by the good works of humaneness which it performs, JAMES seems to have seen that the Hebrew-Christians to whom this epistle was primarily addressed—and the Holy Spirit seems to have seen that those who should read the epistle in subsequent ages—might count words as seeds, as in one sense they really are, and so might turn from good deeds which cost something to words which cost nothing, and so come to have neither an inner life of faith nor outer life of beneficence.

The Hebrew-Christians to whom the epistle was addressed, were peculiarly exposed to this temptation, as the itch for teaching was prevalent among the Israelites in the time of Jesus. In an apocryphal book entitled "The Ascension of Isaiah the Prophet," supposed by its editor, Dr. Lawrence, to have been written near the beginning of the propagation of the Christian faith, there occur these words (ch. 3 : 23, 24), in a passage regarding the Messiah, quoted by Barnes : " In those days shall many be attached to office, destitute of wisdom ; multitudes of iniquitous elders and pastors, injurious to their flocks and addicted to rapine, nor shall the holy pastors themselves diligently discharge their duties."

This must have been most exasperatingly true when the Christ was on earth, or else He could never have uttered that terrific indictment which fills the twenty-third chapter of Matthew, one of the most fearful passages in all the Holy Scriptures, the thunder-burst of whose invective closes with that shower of tenderness, "O Jerusalem, Jerusalem, thou that killest the prophets and stonest them that are sent unto thee, how often would I have gathered thy children together, even as a hen gathereth her chickens under her wings, and ye would not !"

THE TONGUE IN PUBLIC.

When the early churches were formed, the Hebrew-Christians had trouble from this itch of teaching, which led so many incompetent and improper persons to undertake teaching and preaching. Paul found "false apostles, deceitful workers" at Corinth (2 Cor. 11 : 13) ; "dogs, evil workers," in the church at Philippi, which he so loved (Phil. 5: 2), and "false brethren" in the churches of Galatia (Gal. 2). He warns his young brother and friend, Timothy (Tim. 1) against such as had "turned aside to vain jangling, desiring to be teachers of the law, understanding neither what they say nor whereof they affirm." All these are denounced, in the last book of the sacred canon, as being of "the synagogue of Satan" (Rev. 2: 9).

No wonder, then, that the wise JAMES gives special attention to guarding his brethren against becoming conceited, and, having neither faith nor works, supposing that they meet the requirements of religious life by cultivating a dictatorial speech, and putting on magisterial airs.

We may suppose, first of all, that JAMES had reference to those who desired to enter upon the office of public teachers, and whose zeal without knowledge impelled them to places for which they were not prepared. It is a great thing to be a preacher of the Gospel. Every Christian man may well covet it as one of the best gifts. The earnest desire of every Christian parent should be that his boys may be church ministers, and his daughters become the wives of pastors. He should do all he can to prepare them for these positions, if such be the will of God, as indicated by His providence. They will not all become so; but a preparation of spirit for the ministry of the word would be the best preparation for any other position in the Church; and the Lord would lead away from the pulpit to other Christian fields all conscientious Christian men who stood ready to do the Lord's will everywhere, and who selected their positions in the Church not in view of any personal and worldy advantage, but in view of the judgment-seat of Christ.

To that tribunal we are pointed by the word which is translated "condemnation." We all "stand before the judgment-seat of Christ" (Rom. 14:10). If all who are now in the ministry of the word, when deciding what course to pursue, had placed themselves conscientiously before the great Judge, to learn from Him, as shall be learned at the last judgment, whether they should become preachers, may we not in all charity suppose that there are many now preaching who would be doing much more for Christ's work in the world, on farms and wharves, in shops and factories, pleading law or practising physic?

There are those who doubtless will be swift to give an affirmative answer to that question, as there are many who are very ready to find fault with the poverty of the pulpit; but, on the other hand, may not the question be put pointedly to such persons, and to thousands of other men in the Church, who are now in the wrong business, whether, if all worldly considerations had been put aside and they had settled the question in the light of the Christ's white throne of judgment, they would not now be preaching the truth as it is in Christ with power surpassing many who are accredited teachers of the word?

In any case the place of teacher is to be assumed very deliberately and conscientiously in the remembrance that he who receives it receives a great increase of responsibility; and if he fail of his duty, a greater condemnation.

THE TONGUE IN PRIVATE.

But manifestly we should not confine JAMES'S words to public and authorized teachers. They form a very small section of those who were probably in the mind of the writer whose words we are studying. There was a disease prevalent in the Church in the days of JAMES, which, in many places, is a raging epidemic in our own times. It is an internal disease discovered by its eruption, which appears ordinarily on the tongue, and sometimes on the right hand that holds pen or pencil. It proves the presence, in the afflicted individual, of *much-teachingness*, a disposition to be always taking the chair, much given to finding fault, correcting, playing the censor, putting on professional airs, having an opinion on every subject, with great readiness to give it dogmatically, dictatorially, pontifically, as being paramount, final, infallible, from which there is no appeal.

Almost every one must have noticed displays of this in social and business circles, and in religious assemblies, whether met for counsel or worship. It is a dangerous and hurtful habit, to be corrected by those who have formed it and to be avoided by those who have not.

THE GREAT RESPONSIBILITY.

Against it JAMES warns us, first, by the great responsibility taken by its indulgence. If we assume to know enough to teach, we can never plead ignorance when we are called to account. If we should make a mistake, our assumption of superior knowledge will probably lead many astray, and so render our lives increasingly injurious. That is the first reason for not rushing into the teacher's responsibility. Another is, that we all make mistakes. JAMES is very modest. He does not unnecessarily condemn himself. The "we" is conciliatory. He is addressing his brethren. He remembers that he himself is not faultless. A study of one's own manifold frailties of character and temper should make one very careful in reviewing what seems to be the faults of others, and in sitting in judgment upon them. Especially should it guard us against utterance of criticism and judgment.

DANGERS OF THE TONGUE.

This naturally leads to a consideration of the dangers of the tongue, and the evils produced by much speaking. There is no member of the human body so important as the tongue : nor hand, nor foot, nor ear, nor eye. With nothing can we do so much good and so much evil. When a certain ancient king sent an animal to be offered to the gods, he requested that the best and the worst should be returned to him, and the wise priest sent *the tongue* of the victim back to the king.

The heathen philosopher Xanthus, expecting some friends to dine with him, ordered his servant Æsop to provide the best things the market could supply. Tongues only were provided; and these the cook was ordered to serve up with different sauces. Course after course was supplied, each consisting of tongue. "Did I not order you," said Xanthus, in a violent passion, "to buy the best victuals the market afforded?" "And have I not obeyed your orders?" said Æsop. "Is there anything better than a tongue? Is not the tongue the bond of civil society, the organ of truth and reason, and the instrument of our praise and adoration of the gods?" Xanthus ordered him to go again to the market on the morrow, and buy the worst things he could find. Æsop went, and again he purchased tongues, which the cook was ordered to serve as before. "What! tongues again?" exclaimed Xanthus. "Most certainly," rejoined Æsop; "the tongue is surely the worst thing in the world. It is the instrument of all strife and contention, the inventor of lawsuits, and the source of division and wars; it is the organ of error, of lies, calumny and blasphemies."

THE MENTAL TUBERCLE.

Speech is the great good gift. There is a little gland, found only in the human species, called the *mental tubercle*. No animal without that can speak. It is present only with the animal which thinks. What cannot think cannot speak. The ancient Greeks, by using the same word for speech and thought, seem to have anticipated this later discovery; and the modern German was as wise as he was witty when he said, "I will believe that any animal thinks when he *tells* me so."

So close is this connection that JAMES says that any man who neither stumbles in his speech nor causes any one else to stumble, is a perfect man; for the reason that he must be able to control his whole person if he have perfect control over his tongue. And this will be manifest if we consider the following:

(1) That the tongue is the organ for the utterance of thoughts and emotions. That good and not evil may come, that the utterance may be sweet and not bitter, there must be such control of the head and heart as that the bitter bad will be held back in the soul and the sweet good will be sent forward to the tongue.

(2) That the thought and emotion, until the tongue give them utterance, can do no harm outside ourselves. Before utterance they may be revised, corrected, changed; but once uttered, they belong no more to us. The tongue is the Rubi-

con of thought. It is the tongue that gives life and power for good or evil to the thoughts of men.

(3) That the reaction of speech is important. A man may speak so as to soothe himself and increase his own reasonableness, meekness, and sweetness; or, he may lash himself into fury and talk wildly until he becomes wild. We have spoken before of the effect of the tones of the voice on the temper. A quarrel cannot be carried on in dulcet tone.

(4) That the words of a man are the indices of his character. Having no other knowledge of a man, if all he had said and written could be made known to any intelligent being, that person could form a fair estimate of the man's character without any knowledge whatever of his acts. Men cannot see into each other's hearts and minds for evidence of character; they have only what the inner man sends forth. In one sense our words always represent us fairly; we are mistaken if we think they do not. "I did not mean that" may be said when one has misrepresented our words; but in the case where the words are accurately reported as they were uttered, they either conveyed our meaning exactly or they correctly represent our inability at the moment to select the word befitting our thought. He who knows all that is in the mind of God and in the mind of men, uttered a profound and tremendous truth when He said,

" By thy words thou shalt be justified and by thy words thou shalt be condemned " (Matt. 12 : 37). It is worthy of note that He assigned this as the ground of His assertion, " that every idle word that men speak, they shall give account thereof in the day of judgment." So, to make a full and perfect estimate of a man's character, there must not be omitted one single, solitary, slightest word that ever drops from his life or his pen. They must all be gathered by the great *Estimator* in making final judgment on the man's character.

And we are never to forget that, whatever importance is to be attached to either words or deeds in this world, in that other state of existence, upon which we are to enter at death, character is everything. As a man speaks so are his thoughts, and "as he thinketh in his heart, so is he" (Prov. 13 : 7).

A PERFECT MAN.

In view of all these truths, how thoroughly is our author justified in taking the ground, that when a man shows perfect control over his tongue he has control over his head, and his heart, and his whole personality.

This may seem to be a great thing to say to so small a member as the tongue. But the writer of this epistle sustains the position, not by any arguments drawn from metaphysics, but by illustrations appealing to our common sense.

(1) From animate things he selects the horse. It is a powerful animal. A horse's bit is a small thing, and yet when put in the unruly horse's mouth, we can control him better therewith than if he had much harness fastened to every limb, and worked by much machinery. So, he who controls his tongue controls his naturally unruly body.

(2) From inanimate objects he selects the ships. A ship is vast; not being unruly as the horse is, it is, however, driven by fierce winds. What a great power would be required to pull it against the face of the storm. In our day there is an immense steamship called the Great Eastern. A force applied from without to change its position, would be that of many thousands of horse-power; and yet, when that huge mass of material and machinery is beaten upon by winds, travelling at the rate of many miles an hour, a little rudder changes its direction or holds it to its course. One single small man at the helm can so work the machinery that his rudder will instantly change the position of a vast hulk, which a thousand men could not budge.

The tongue is like that horse and needs the "bit," and like that ship and needs the "rudder." "It rears and charges like a proud horse," seems to be the meaning of JAMES, when he says that it "boasts greatly." And well it may. More than sceptres and swords, more than bayonets and cannon, more than steam and electricity, is one single human tongue. This day, while I write (29 March, 1889), there is one tongue in Europe, in a poor, sick mouth, whose sweet utterances are keeping Europe in Easter peace. A hundred words from that tongue would, in a hundred hours, change the values of all properties in Christendom, and in a hundred days array millions of human beings in hostility, and change the face of affairs in all the continents and islands of the world. May not a member which can do such great things, boast itself of great things?

THE TONGUE AND THE PEN.

We are never to forget the "tongue" includes the "pen." No creature writes that does not think, and no creature thinks that cannot talk, if its organs be perfect. It is not the mere instrumental tongue or instrumental pen. It is the *word*. Words are things, as much as bullets and daggers, and often are just as killing. Once, a New York paper gave an account of the terrible fall of a very beautiful woman. There was no reason of justice, or mercy, or public utility, or private help, to be had by publishing the facts, with the names, but they were startlingly sensational. That woman's widowed mother, who, in a distant land, had reared a large family most respectably, whose other children are doing well, received a marked copy of the paper, detailing sickeningly the degradation of her child, and in a day that mother became a lunatic, and a whole circle were made to suffer under the redoubled blows of the affliction. The reporter who caught up that morsel of scandal, and the publisher of that paper who unnecessarily paraded it to the world, and the person who sent that marked copy to the poor mother, are guilty before God for that old lady's lunacy and the many heart-breaks that followed.

It may be well to notice especially the case of the person sending the marked copy. There are people who are never heard to make vocal utterances that damage or even disparage others, who nevertheless fancy it no harm to send anonymous notes injuring the reputation of others, provided they be persuaded that what they state is the fact, or to send a marked article in a paper which they know will give pain, supposing that the writer is responsible for the truth of the statement. It is proper that such persons should be taught the common-sense morality of Christianity.

First of all, it must be borne in mind, that while it is *always wrong* to tell a lie for any purpose, it is *not* always right to utter a truth. Indeed, it is a question whether it is not always wrong to utter any truth *without any purpose*. We are always to "speak the truth in love" (Eph. 4 : 15). Whatever we speak, or otherwise publish, must be truth. But, what we know as truth, is to be published or communicated to another only for reasons prompted by our love for God or for man. If my duty to any fellow-creature demand my utterance of anything that is true, I must utter it, although the wrong-doer suffer thereby. The same holds good when my sense of duty to the public is concerned.

A PUBLISHER'S RESPONSIBILITY.

The publisher of a journal is bound to announce the wrong of any official, when it becomes certified to him. This duty is created by his patriotism. But if he make the charge without *knowing* it to be true, he is a liar and a slanderer. He does not become less a liar and a slanderer, if it afterward turn out that the damaging allegation was true. He intended to publish it, true or false. True or false as the statement may be, he is as guilty as the author. He would have invented it if he could. He "*took* up a reproach against his neighbor" (Ps. 15 : 3). Invention requires some genius; any fool can convey a slander.

But the statements of social conversation and of the press sometimes concern private individuals. Then we have no right to publish the wrongs we know, unless compelled thereto by the law of justice or the law of benevolence. If I see that a man whom I know to be a seducer, is making advances to the daughter of another man, I am bound to go to the father and furnish him the facts in my possession. But I must not go to others and say "Isn't it a pity that Mr. A. lets that Mr. B. wait on his daughter, when B. is such a licentious man?" I have no right to slander Mr. A. by supposing that he knowingly exposes his daughter's morals to danger. I have no right to soil the good name of the innocent Miss A., who may thus always thereafter be injured by being known as "that girl who had something to do with that dirty Mr. B."

Little as against great! A spark is so small beside a hundred acres of pine forest that no fractional expression can impart an idea of the comparison. And yet, a spark dropped from a man's pipe has destroyed hundreds of thousands of valuable trees. And the tongue is a fire, and a word is a spark. Is the world vast? The tongue of man is a world. It can say all that all the world can think. It can describe all that all the world has done or can do. It is the tongue that directs the world. It is what men say which governs what men do. There is so much evil in the organ of speech that it is well called "a *world* of iniquity."

More evil has been done by the tongue than by all man's other organs and members. When the heart is not right, when it is like those mirrors which distort every object presented, then the tongue multiplies the copies of the deformed image, and society is filled with uglinesses.

SATAN'S TONGUE.

Satan knows that if he could rule every tongue he would rule the world. He does his mischief by his tongue. No man probably ever sees or feels him with the hand. But he kills many a man. He has no dagger, no spear, no sword, no gun. But he has a tongue, and God declares that he is a murderer and a liar. And that he may make murderers and liars, he sets men's tongues on fire. He murders with his lying tongue, and men and women similarly commit murder. Yes, "and women." Sometimes, words that blister, and bite, and kill, fall from beautiful lips, whose honey-sweetness conceals tongues "full," as our author says, "of death-bearing poison." And those words kill as surely as if spit from between the snaggled teeth of an obscene old witch.

When inflamed, the wicked tongue does two things. (1) It hurts the evil speaker. It reacts upon him, increasing his envy, jealousy, hatred or whatever evil passion prompted the bad speech. No, sir, you are mistaken if you think to destroy your neighbor by your tongue and escape unharmed yourself. No, madam, you cannot deliberately smirch your sister's reputation, however bad a woman she may be, without making yourself a worse woman. Perhaps those very facts in her history which you are using to her injury may not be so bad, nor inspired by so vicious a spirit as that temper which prompts you to go about, scattering damaging reports concerning her. At any rate, every unkind speech leaves the speaker worse. Not causelessly did the wise Solomon say, "Suffer not thy mouth to cause thy flesh to sin" (Eccles. 5:6).

(2) It hurts others. It arouses suspicions against them. It blocks up the way of their return to virtue if they be bad. If they be innocent it tries and condemns them without a hearing. What is said against a man in his absence he cannot disprove. He knows nothing of it. He might be able to exculpate himself thoroughly if he heard the allegation. But he is cut off from that right. An evil report against a person may spread a long time without his knowledge. People who look at him suspiciously, may innocently misinterpret the actions they see, and thus have their suspicions confirmed. It is well known that if the man with the healthiest mind among men should go to a small town in which all the inhabitants believed him insane, the simplest and most natural actions would seem to them confirmations of the theory of his insanity.

And, then, such things spread, like a fire which the Indians used to kindle on the prairies, when a spark from flint and steel would sweep through the dry grass so fiercely and so rapidly, that men and horses were compelled to flee for their lives over weary miles or fall and perish in the flames.

THE ONE UNTAMABLE THING.

How untamable is the tongue! It began in Eden. It has been at its dreadful work of uttering filth, lies, and slanders ever since. Men have tamed lions, and tigers, and wolves, birds of prey and poisonous snakes, and even the fish of the sea—but "the tongue of men hath no man subdued." Why can it not be done? Because it is the "tongue of men," the *human* tongue; because it is not mere animal's. Human nature can subdue animal nature, but who is to subdue the devilish nature, when it takes possession of human nature? The tongue can never be subdued; to be useful, it must be made the organ of a renewed, regenerated, transformed spirit. In itself it is an "unrestrainable evil, full of death-bearing poison."

RELIGIOUS USES OF THE TONGUE.

And so JAMES leads us to think of the religious use of the tongue, and the protest which religion makes against slander. The existence of the gift of speech, together with its restriction to man and its connection with the capability of reasoning, is a very powerful theistic argument. For such a gift men should be naturally grateful. And there can be nothing found by which men can praise God for the gift of the tongue but the tongue itself. How great, therefore, is the sin, when the tongue is used to insult God. Nothing is so dear to God as man. There is no man on earth, however low, who is not dearer to God than any angel, for no angel is His child, and God, who has been "found in fashion as a man," has never worn angelic nature. So, he who slanders or curses a man, insults God, as he who spits upon the statue of the Emperor, insults the majesty of the Empire.

There is no necessity for those things. All nature is against them. From a fountain must issue fresh water or salt. Any saltness, however little, spoils the freshness. Any bitterness of speech spoils the stream which proceeds out of the heart through the mouth. The drink is not wholesome, although there be but one drop of poison to a pint of the purest water that ever welled up from the clearest spring through bowl of granite rock. There is no double-dealing in nature. It would be idle to seek olives on a fig tree or figs on a grape-vine. We should not expect to find a devil's fruit on a God's tree! This thing would not be, if every man gave his life wholly to the service of God. The sweetened heart would make the language sweet, and every speech uttered regarding man would sound in echo like a shout to God.

SOURCE OF THE EVIL.

Having so forcibly pointed out the evils of an unruly tongue, JAMES indicates the sources of that evil in the bad passions of the human heart which incite men to desire to be considered wiser than they are. This naturally leads to envy, and that to malice. *Wisdom* is to be desired, not the mere *reputation of wisdom*. And there is a true wisdom and a false. And our author makes a contrast between them in their origin, their characteristics, and their effects. These are his words (chap. 3 : 13–18) : *" Who is wise and intelligent among you? Let him show out of a good life his works in meekness of wisdom. But if you have bitter zeal and party-spirit in your heart, do not boast, and do not be against the truth. This is not that wisdom coming down from above, but is earthly, sensuous, demoniacal. For where jealousy and party-spirit, there anarchy and every foul deed. But the wisdom from above is first hallowed, then peaceable, reasonable, persuadable, full of compassion and good fruits, not sectarian, not hypocritical. And the fruit of righteousness in peace is sown by them that make peace."*

In studying the epistle now before us, we are to bear in mind that it was addressed to Hebrew-Christians, to persons who had been Jews at a fanatical period of Jewish history, and who still must have retained much of the violent spirit of their old associations, and who had not yet been filled with the spirit of our Lord. This will explain the tenor of the letter, and the form of its phraseology, and not deprive us of those lessons in morality which we are seeking from its pregnant sentences and phrases.

Our author's advice regarding the selection of public teachers is, that a man shall have wisdom, intelligence and usefulness. The absence of any one of these from his life should be considered fatal to his claims for so high, so responsible, so important an office as that of teacher. Has he gifts? Has he grace? Has he fruit? These are the three questions.

"WISDOM AND KNOWLEDGE."

It must be observed that there is a difference between wisdom and knowledge. One is natural, the other acquired; one comes from God, the other from man. A man who is not wise cannot acquire wisdom by his own exertions; but any man can become learned, if he have industry and memory. A man may be wise and unlearned; a man may be learned and be a fool. Wisdom is as superior to learning as the man who is both architect and builder is superior to the materials which he uses. But as those materials are necessary to the builder, so is learning to a wise man. Therefore, he who is truly wise will industriously seek to obtain all knowledge within his reach. No man to whom God has given wisdom despises learning. He can do little without it. It is that with which he is to make his life-work. The very first motion of wisdom in a man, is to "get understanding," to obtain a knowledge of things.

From the very first these two were required in those who were to rule and lead in the Church of

God. Moses called upon the Israelities to choose men who were (1) wise, (2) intelligent, and (3) known; and such men he would appoint to be their rulers (Deut. 1 : 13). The basis of all is wisdom, the implement of wisdom is intelligence, and the result of the combination will produce that which makes a man known among his fellows.

It is idle for a man to undertake to prove that he is wise. He may declaim and argue. But what has he *done?* When the country needs a chief magistrate, a candidate being a great orator is almost no recommendation ! What has he *done?* is the natural question. What great measure of statesmanship has he originated, or conspicuously forwarded, or consummated? If none of these exist, no gift of speech, no magnetism of manner, no shrewd political combinations will avail to advance his claim. And if there exist in his history those fruits which are the product of wisdom and intelligence, and of wisdom and intelligence only, they will be seen, and make him known. The more men talk against his good deeds the more conspicuous will those good deeds become.

JAMES, therefore, intimates that if a man is to be selected for wisdom, he cannot make manifest that wisdom by an argument to prove its existence, but all he has to do is to show from a good life, a life of truth, fidelity and beneficence, that he has so used what he has acquired as to adapt all objects in his control to their intended end. Not only by words but by works let the world see his wisdom, not only in one field but in all fields, not only on one side of his character, but on all sides let all who know anything of him know that it is good, and let him not parade this, let him show no exultation when it is discovered nor distressful disappointment when it is neglected, and by that very meekness men will be sure that he has wisdom. Meekness may not always be wise, but wisdom is always meek. So the really wise man who is meek impresses us as being more trustworthy than the violent, arrogant, and dictatorial person, who is always striving to secure the reputation of being wise.

So we are turned in upon our hearts. If we have bitter zeal, such a partisan spirit as will allow no good on the other side, a spirit of contentious ambition, we need not attempt to secure our ends by boasting of our qualifications for the part of public teacher; our very spirit would show how devoid we are of such qualifications. A man lies against the truth when he seeks any station of responsible trust and influence which he knows he would never obtain if everyone knew the whole truth as to his character and history.

TWO WISDOMS.

Do you call that wisdom which is so fierce, so vindictive? It is such wisdom as man may acquire, but it is not real wisdom; it has not come as God's gift, but as Satan's training in civil life. It makes a man smart, sharp, cunning; in civil life it may make him a politician, but not a statesman; it may make him an agitator in the Church, but not a leader and a helper. It is not from above. It is from beneath. It may win the admiration of slender wits and malicious spirits, but it will not secure the respect of the good and the intelligent. It is earthly, sensuous, demoniacal. It has no principle, no motive, no end, beyond this present world. It has its rise in the animal nature of man, by which he is akin to the snake and the tiger; and finds its most desired result in the gratification of the lust of the eye, the lust of the flesh, and the pride of life. Its inspiration is that of all evil spirits, *pride*, which is the damnation of Satan (1 Tim. 3:6), and which betrays the soul into maliciousness and makes it the accuser of the brethren. Let all censorious people remember that the devil gets his name from being the accuser of the brethren (Rev. 12:10). Such a one is not the archangel Michael, who might have brought many a truthful accusation against the devil; but even in contest with Diabolus, Michael would not say what might bring him on a level with the worst spirit in the universe. (Jude, 9).

THE WISDOM FROM ABOVE.

With this wisdom, which is only cunning, which is earthly, sensuous, infernal, which is anarchical and destructive, JAMES contrasts that other wisdom, the real and worthy wisdom.

Its origin is different. It is from above. It comes down from the Father of lights and of spirits (1 : 17). The devil never inspires it; he could not. It is not gained from man; he has it not. It is God's direct gift. It must be sought from Him (1 : 5). He gives it. It is such a gift as He bestows on archangels. Against the three lines describing devilish cunning, *earthly*, SENSUOUS, DEMONIAC, are set these seven colors of the light of wisdom, as they come out through the prism of the sanctified common-sense of the brother of Him in whom they blended, and shone, and glowed, until man saw the splendor of God in the beautiful life of the White Christ.

ITS CHARACTERISTICS.

(1) It is hallowed. On the spirit of man who has it there has fallen a sacred hush, as on a temple which a god inhabits. Its precincts are consecrated to worship. All desecrating principles, maxims, thoughts, purposes are excluded. It has no doubtful expedients and utters no words of double-meaning. It is clear, because it has been clarified. It is open to heaven and earth without concealments. It is chaste, seeking no unholy pleasures.

We should lose much if we failed to notice that the first line in this spectrum has reference to the heart. Men so often begin their notions of religion as if it had something to do primarily with the head, making a system of orthodox theology stand for an experience of true religion; whereas, glorious as the true science of theology is, a man may be a very wise man and most profoundly religious before he has so much as heard that there is such a thing as a science called theology. The seat of true wisdom is in the heart. With the head (the intellect) man believes to science, that is, understanding; but with the heart (the emotional part of his nature) man believes to religion, that is, *wisdom*. Paul never uttered a profounder philosophical truth than when he said, "With the heart man believeth unto righteousness" (Romans 10:10). The right heart is always working to make the right head; but the contrary is not true, as many a man has become more wicked as he became more learned, while no man has grown more stupid as he grew purer in heart.

One can easily perceive how the contentious Hebrew-Christians would take this phrase, "first pure," and use it as an excuse for the indulgence of a fierce, fanatical, polemic spirit, claiming that the first duty of the Church was to exterminate heretics and so keep the doctrinal system pure. This were a mad perversion. There is probably nothing written on this passage more profitable to remember than the words of Albert Barnes, here transcribed: "This passage should not be applied, as it often is, to the doctrines of religion, as if it were the first duty of a Church to keep itself free from errors in doctrine, and that this ought to be sought even in preference to the maintenance of peace, as if it meant that in doctrine a Church should be *first* pure *then* peaceable, but it should be applied *to the individual consciences of men* as showing the effect of religion on the heart and life. It is true that a Church should be pure in doctrinal belief, but that is not the truth taught here. It is not true that the Scripture teaches, here or elsewhere, that purity of doctrine is to be preferred to a peaceful spirit; or that it always leads to a peaceful spirit; or that it is proper for professed Christians and Christian ministers to sacrifice, as is often done, a peaceful spirit in an attempt to preserve purity of doctrine. Most of the persecutions in the Church have grown out of this maxim. This led to the establishment of the Inquisition; this kindled the fires of Smithfield; this inspired Laud and his friends; this has been the origin of no small part of the schisms in the Church. A pure spirit is the best promoter of peace, and will do more than anything else to secure the prevalence of truth."

(2) The wisdom which comes from God is peaceable. It is peaceable because it is pure. Men that have no false and wicked purposes cannot break the peace. The peace of the world never has been broken by a pure man, a man

who had no worldly, sensuous, or demoniac desires to gratify. There never was dissension between two friends, never a rupture in any Church, never a rebellion in any State, never a war between two countries, never a wicked controversy of any kind which did not have its origin in some impurity of soul. It is always foolish, as well as wicked, to break the peace. However in our wounded self-love, we may find excuses for our own participation in such transactions, it is certain that in causing, or in aiding to continue, a violation of the peace we are not wise.

Here again we have JAMES echoing the words of his adored brother Jesus: "Blessed are the peace-makers, for they shall be called the children of God" (Matt. 5 : 9). There is no blessing for those who break the peace; there is no blessing for the warriors who fight on the side which breaks the peace. Men may parade them in their short-lived histories, and erect statues to keep before men the effigies of their personality, but they are the children of the devil. However they may fail in their earnest and honest efforts, the peace-makers are always regarded by the Lord of all life as His own children.

And it may be worth noticing that the benediction which, in the Sermon on the Mount, Jesus pronounces on the peace-makers, follows immediately after that which is given to the pure in heart; just as JAMES says: "First pure, then peaceable." Is this a mere coincidence, or has it some logical basis? Can we live in peace without being pure? The pure in heart see God. God is the "Lord of peace" (2 Thess. 3: 16), and gives peace to His children. All dissensions and wars come from the evil in men's hearts, and when that is banished there is no desire for conflict.

(3) This wisdom is *reasonable*. It is not violent in its maintenance of its own convictions; it is not stubborn, unwilling to hear what may be said "on the other side." There are men who deem themselves wise, who storm out what they believe to be the truth. Real wisdom does not so. Where there is a sober conviction of the right, and a firm faith in the final triumph of the right, all that a man has to do is to speak the truth in love. It is folly to hate the men who hold the other view. A wise man pities his opponent, but does not hate him. Hatred would imply something *personal*. The truly wise man does not so much love himself as he loves the truth. If any man hold an error the wise man regards him as most unfortunate, and pities him, as a man in good health pities his neighbor whose eruptions show that he is diseased.

Gentleness is not weak, and is not the product of weakness. It comes from being reasonable. None but the strong can be gentle; others may be soft and apathetic, but gentleness as much requires strength for its basis as the beautiful flowers and verdure require the strong ground of the geological formations. A gentle man gains by giving. He is not punctilious of his rights. He will maintain them, but always on grounds of reason, not of passion. He holds to his property not because it is *his*, but for the reason that he is responsible for it. Just so a man who has this wisdom from above, will not be violent in argument. He maintains his opinions not because they are *his* opinions, but because he has formed them reasonably, and must maintain them reasonably and not passionately. So he will hear what others have to say. He may have had some flaw in his reasoning ; he desires above all things to be right. There may be something against his opinions which he has never thought of ; if there be he wishes to know it. He will listen patiently to an unlettered servant, to a little child, to any one who can contribute in the slightest to the enlargement of his understanding. A man may be weak and soft by nature, but not gentle ; that comes from wisdom, and wisdom comes from without, comes from above. JAMES had already said, "If any of you lack wisdom, let him ask of God, who giveth" (1 : 5). No man is born a gentle man. Such a character is the product of wisdom, and wisdom is not natural, it is the gift of God. We must always keep that in mind. The schools may give culture, learning and other human things, but not wisdom. That comes supernaturally. Solomon was no product of evolution, else some of his descendants would have equalled him, and others would have surpassed him. "He asked of God" (1 Kings 3). "And God gave Solomon wisdom" (1 Kings 4 : 29). "And Solomon's wisdom excelled . . . all the wisdom of Egypt" (1 Kings 4 : 29). Of course it did, because the wisdom of Egypt was only the skill and cunning which human nature can afford, while Solomon's was the true wisdom of celestial origin. [Notice the connection of statements in 1 Kings 5 : 12, "And the Lord gave Solomon *wisdom* as He had promised Him ; and there was *peace* between Hiram and Solomon."]

(4) This wisdom is *persuadable*. Our author here uses a word which is not found elsewhere in the Holy Scripture, and which cannot be fully rendered, perhaps, by any single word in the English tongue. It certainly does not indicate any deficiency of character, and surely those who are easily influenced for others, whose nature is sometimes described as "a nose of wax," have no right to this epithet. "Easily persuaded?" Well, yes: if that mean that he stands open to conviction, willing to listen, free from stubbornness; but not if it mean that he is carried everywhere and anywhere by all the winds that blow. As the word which we have translated "reasonable" (in the Common Version "gentle")

indicates the condition of the wise man's soul when he is striving to convince others, so this "persuadable" seems to indicate the posture of his soul when others are striving to convince him. It means that if he has made an error he will not keep wandering on because he is unwilling to retrace his steps by the same path. It means that he will not waste energy in endeavoring to hold an untenable position under the control of intellectual pride. It means that he can be won over by fair means and sound argument. He yields to no force that is not reasonable, as he employs no agency that is not reasonable.

There are persons, as we all know, who have no sign of this characteristic of wisdom, and ordinarily, when this is absent, so is this third characteristic, "reasonableness." They are twin virtues. He who seeks to win over his opponent only by fair means, is very liable to be easily won by fair means.

We are to remember that this epistle was addressed to those whose ruling fault was contentiousness. They were contending for that which was ready to perish. They were holding out for old rules against new principles. They were striving to put the new wine of Christianity into a ritual which was an old bottle JAMES points out the unwisdom of this, that it was the folly of those who preferred the bottle to the wine.

(5) The fifth trait of heavenly wisdom is *compassion*, "which," Josephus says, "of good passions was most of all lost among Jews." Here, again, we have an echo of the teachings of JAMES'S brother, Jesus, in the Sermon on the Mount: "Blessed are the merciful, for they shall obtain mercy" (Matt. v). In a man of true celestial wisdom there is so much sympathy and compassion that it is perpetually bursting out into fruits of goodness, which are so profitable that all men acknowledge them. You cannot know so well the condition of the tree, but fruits are visible and palpable. Men know the tree by the fruit, as God knows the fruit by the tree.

(6) Sectarianism is the pride of the sectary, but the humiliation of all true religion. The wisdom from above does not lessen a man's love for his own denomination, but it enlarges his love for the good of all denominations. It avoids confining all the good to one good thing. It does not abandon its own Church, but it belongs to all other Churches, and they all belong to it.

The word here is not confined to religious circles, but has the widest meaning. Wherever this heavenly wisdom goes, it avoids bringing upon itself the condemnation of being "partial," and "a judge of evil thoughts" (2:4). It is not partisan. It will not adhere to a party it loves, "right or wrong." It will not condemn the other party, "wrong or right." It will not oppress the poor when it happens to be rich, nor wrong the rich when it happens to be poor. Appeals on grounds of caste or, class, or previous condition will have no effect upon its judgment. It regards a man for what he is, not for what he has, or has been.

The Jews, at the time of Christ, accounted themselves as the only "people"; all other nations being "dogs" and so unclean that they were not to be admitted to social intercourse. This partiality was carried to such an extreme of sectarianism as even to override their greed for gain; for it was regarded as disgraceful to trade with the Gentiles. This so impressed other nations, that Tacitus said of the Jews that "they would be merciful to men of their own religion and country, but hated all mankind besides." Their bitter feeling to Samaritans is the key to the conversation which the woman of Samaria had with our Lord at Jacob's well (John 4), and to our Lord's parable of the Good Samaritan. (Luke 10).

When some of them became Christians the old spirit broke forth in sectarianism. Some desired to keep the old Judaism; others were for the fullest enjoyment of the liberty wherewith the Christ had made them free. Some were for war with Rome; others were for peace. The latter were regarded by the former as no better than heathen. JAMES points out to his brethren, how utterly wanting in heavenly wisdom was all this fiery, fierce fanaticism. Well had it been for the Jews of his day if they had heeded his words of prudent and godly common-sense. Their sectarianism produced the rebellions which precipitated their destruction.

(7) The last characteristic of the heavenly wisdom mentioned by our author, is the absence of all hypocrisy. Hypocrisy was a crying sin among the Jews. Against nothing did Jesus the Christ lift up His voice in more clear and terrible notes than against hypocrisy. In strain after strain of terrific invective He denounced it to scribe and pharisee and publican and sinner and disciple, with woe upon woe upon woe, as if He would reduplicate and multiply its damnation.

A CHEERING PROMISE.

The whole passage closes with a most charming and cheering promise. If the teachers and professors of the faith of the Lord Jesus will *cultivate* peace—not simply do occasional acts—they will be as men who sow good seed, which shall bring them a plentiful harvest. It will be a harvest after the kind of the seed sown. It will be "peace in righteousness." It will not be that poor peace which a man temporarily enjoys in return for the sacrifice of some principle, and which is always followed by unrest. It will be "peace in righteousness." Whatever others may do to them, whatever calumnies and slanders may be uttered against them, they that have not spoken bitter and slanderous words will know peace. And that peace will be permanent. The gains of strife are bitter fruits, as well to him who gains as to him that loses thereby. But the fruits of "peace in righteousness" shall be eternal.

It is delightful to trace the echoes of the words of Jesus in the words of JAMES. "Blessed are the peace-makers, for they shall be called the children of God," said the one (Matt. 5:9), and "the fruit of peace in righteousness," says the other, "is sown by them that make peace." And of old time, the Psalmist said (Ps. 97:11), "Light is sown for the righteous," and the prophet (Isa. 32:17), declared that "the work of righteousness is peace, and the effect of righteousness, quietness and assurance forever."

VIII.

Demoniacal Wisdom.

CHAPTER IV., 1-3.

FRUITS OF DEMONIAC WISDOM.

IN the opening of the fourth chapter, JAMES points his readers to the terrible fruits of that wisdom which is not from above, but is earthly, sensuous, and demoniacal.

"*Whence wars and whence fightings among you? Are they not hence, even from your pleasures exerting their force in your members? You strongly desire and have not; you slay and are zealous, and you are not able to obtain. You fight and war, and have not, because you pray not. You ask and do not receive, because you pray wickedly, that you may spend it on your pleasures.*"

Those Jews who had become Christians, were in a large measure moved by that unrest which agitated those who still remained under the old ritual of religion. Among the former it was the tares sown among the wheat. Among the latter it was as a field all overgrown with tares. Readers of the New Testament will recollect allusions to this state of affairs in the Gospels and in the Acts of the Apostles. The Jewish people were looking for the Messiah, not because He stood for the salvation of their souls, and the elevation of the moral tone of the people, but as for One who should lead them against the Roman force, and with superhuman power break the Roman yoke. Questions connected with the main issue, or arising therefrom, divided households and inflamed neighborhoods. The coming of Jesus, and the hopes which were at first begotten by His advent, and then disappointed by the pacific turn of His ministry, increased the popular inflammation. Pretenders and seditious scoundrels, and perhaps sincere fanatics were taking advantage of this heated expectation, to add fuel to the flame. In the twenty-fourth chapter of Matthew Jesus warns His disciples against those who should claim to be the political Christ. If they were solicited to follow some leader to the desert, or join some secret cabal in the city (v. 26) they were not to be drawn into peril by listening to such calls, for the reason that the coming of the true Messiah would be with as unmistakable a sign as the flash of the lightning. The Jewish people were themselves in parties on this question, some carrying their spirit of resistance to Rome into violent procedure, in which they were opposed by those who hated Rome no less, but counselled moderation as more prudent. Then, when some of them became Christians, those who remained Jews fought them. Then those Christians were divided among themselves, some leaning to the old ritual, some insisting violently on the old ritual, some opposing all re-Judaizing tendencies, and zealously, and sometimes violently, fighting for the freedom of the Gospel, some for the spiritual freedom of the new form of faith, and some for what was so great a perversion of Christian freedom that it was little less than licentiousness.

FALSE CHRISTS.

Three years before the beginning of the Christian era, there had arisen a false Messiah, named Theudas, and, subsequently, "in the days of the taxing," had arisen one Judas of Galilee, who led forth a band of four hundred men, all of whom the Romans had destroyed (Acts 5). And yet, so great was the hatred of Rome, and so fixed were the Jews in the opinion that the Messiah was to be a temporal prince, who should deliver them from the Roman yoke, that down to the writing of this epistle, broils, tumults, and seditions, all unsuccessful, marked the history of the Jewish people, in every city, as Josephus says, not only in Judea, but in Alexandria, Syria, and many others places.

It is quite easy to conceive that the excellent writer of this epistle had in his mind the intent to reach the Jews who were outside the circle of Hebrew-Christians by this letter, which was primarily addressed to those brethren and circulating among them, and thus contribute what he could to postpone, if he could not avert, the destruction of his people by the superior power of the Romans.

EVILS OF WAR.

What a tremendous and a terrific thing is war! How it makes one shudder to read the blood-red pages of the history of humanity from the beginning. Some sketch of the havoc of war is found in the following statement by Burton: "The siege of Troy lasted ten years, eight months. It is said there died 870,000 Grecians, 670,000 Trojans; at the taking of the city were slain 276,000 men, women, and children of all sorts. Cæsar killed a million, Mohammed the second Turk, 30,000; Curius Dentatus fought in a hundred battles; eight times in single combat he overcame, had forty wounds, was rewarded with one hundred and forty crowns, triumphed nine times for his various services. M. Sergius had thirty-two wounds; Scæva the Centurion, I know not how many; every nation hath their Hectors, Cæsars, and Alexanders. Our [English] Edward the Fourth was in twenty-six battles afoot; and as they do all, he glories in it; this is related to his honor. At the siege of Jerusalem, 1,100,000 died with sword and famine. At the battle of Cannæ, 70,000 men were slain, as Polybius records, and as many at the Battle Abbey with us [in England]; and it is no news to fight from sun to sun, as they did, as Constantine, Licinius, etc. At the siege of Ostend, a poor town in respect, a small fort, but a great grave, 120,000 men lost their lives, besides whole towns ruined, and hospitals full of maimed soldiers. There were engines, fireworks, and whatsoever the devil could invent to do mischief, with 2,500,000 iron bullets, and shot of forty pounds weight, three or four millions of gold consumed."

The following figures are taken from the statistics of the Franco-German war, published by the Prussian War Office. In August, 1870, 780,728 German soldiers crossed the French frontier, followed, during the war, by 222,762 others. The soldiers remaining in Germany were 400,000. At the close of the armistice the German army counted 936,618 men. The army besieging Paris numbered 180,000, while the Paris garrison numbered 230,000 men. The number of combats in which at least one company, one squadron, or a battery was engaged was 766. 333,341 French prisoners were sent into Germany. The French lost 107 flags, 7,441 cannon, and 855,000 firearms. The loss of the German army was 129,000 men, of whom 40,862 were killed, and 88,838 wounded; 17,572 were killed on the field, and 10,710 died in consequence of their wounds. The battle of Gravelotte cost 20,159 men; Mars-la-Tour, 15,790; Woerth, 10,642; Sedan, 9,924; the siege of Paris, 12,509; and Metz, 5,571. The number of shots from field guns was 362,662. The soldiers used 30,000,000 cartridges, the most being by the Third Corps at Mars-la-Tour, where 720,000 rifle shots were fired, and the batteries fired 10,000 grenades.

The loss of life would be appalling, if that were all that war entailed. But it is not. Among those who die in battle are many who are a good riddance to the world. The place of the better portion is soon taken by the successive generations of men. The killing is not all. The bitterness infused into society by the intrigues and plottings that precede wars, the heart-burnings of the authors of wars, the desolation of homes, the long-drawn agonies of fathers and mothers and wives and daughters and friends of the men who are called to the field, the great army of widows and orphans they leave, the vast destruction of property, which can be replaced only by years of great toil, and the legacies of troubles, taxes, debts, and political bitterness, bequeathed to survivors, are added elements of distress.

When all this is surveyed, a thoughtful mind naturally wonders how human nature can so much as allow war, not to say glory in war. And yet there is the fact, that even at the close of the nineteenth century after all the forms of religion, true and false, have been seen in the world from the beginning; after Christianity, the religion of the strongest and greatest personality that ever appeared amongst men, a Man who died rather than fight or even lend Himself to a warlike party or purpose, a religion which has stimulated and aided the intellectual advancement of the race and produced all its civilization that is worth anything, after all its centuries of influence—there remains the fact, that, at this day, millions of men are drawn from the profitable labors of peace to the devastating employments of war, or are standing in idle array awaiting the onset of battle, while their clothes, their arms, their defences, their support, must be wrung from the other millions who are allowed to stay at home, only because the army must be supported.

Surely, in our age, we may heed the sharp cry of JAMES, "Whence came wars and fightings among you?" We do well to bow to the instruction of this wise teacher, who turns us in upon our hearts for an answer, "Are they not hence, even from your pleasures exerting their force in your members?"

The rhetorical movement of speaking to his brethren, and through them to others, as if they were present gives great vivacity to the style of our author. Those whom he addressed, were perfectly well aware of the warlike spirit of the people, which was productive of "fightings among" individuals. He does not say one word as against war, as that was not needed. "Wars and fightings" always mean wickedness and wretchedness. It is not a question whether war be bad or not. None but a diabolical intellect would undertake to frame an argument in defence of war in the abstract. It is an admitted dire evil. Whence comes it? There is no other spring of such a baleful stream than that which is found in the human heart.

WHENCE COME WARS.

"Whence wars and whence fightings among you? Are they not hence, even from your pleasures, which war in your members?" The word here translated "pleasures" is used to express the pleasure of the senses, and hence sometimes signifies strong desire for such gratification. In this picturesque sentence, these are represented as warriors spreading themselves through "the members," seizing the body as the instrument for the accomplishing of their designs and the gaining of their ends. It is the desire for greater territories, larger incomes, more splendor, wider indulgence in physical pleasures, greater gratification of their pride and ambition, which lead kings to war. Every war has begun in sin.

It is so in religious circles. The pride of opinion, the love of rule, the enjoyment of more renown for numbers and wealth and influence, have led sects and Churches into all the persecution and so-called religious wars which have disgraced the cause of truth, and discouraged the aspirations of the good, and increased the infidelity of the world.

Appealing to the Jews JAMES calls their attention vividly to their moral and spiritual condition,

"You strongly desire and have not." [Here the word translated "lust" is not of the same root as the word so translated in the preceding verse]. Whitby points out that the lusting of the Jews of that day was after two things: (1) Liberty— freedom from that tribute which was the token of their subjection. Josephus says that they were continually clamoring for this, "to have the tributes taken away"; and that the *Zealots*, "the band of thieves and their magicians were still pressing the people to fight for their liberty from the Roman yoke." (2) They lusted not only for freedom, but for domination over other peoples. The desire for independence had its basis in good, although it led them to do wicked things to secure it. They desired to bring other people into the galling relation to themselves which they were suffering in their relation to the Romans. And what was true politically was true ecclesiastically. They desired to rule others, the unchristianized Jews striving to dominate the Hebrew-Christians, and they striving in return against the Jews, while the latter were looking for a Messiah who should enable them to tyrannize the heathen.

THE FRUITLESSNESS OF SIN.

How fruitless all this wicked exertion! "What you desire you have not," says JAMES. "You slay and are enemies; yet, even in such extreme measures, you have not the power to obtain what you want. You have slain John the Baptist.

You have slain the Lord of life and glory. You have slain that good man Stephen. You have slain James Zebedee. You have endeavored to slay Paul!" What an indictment! And how short a time after it was uttered was it before they slew the author of this epistle himself.

And yet had they gained anything? A few proselytes were made from one sect to another: that was all. What a poor purchase at what a prodigious price! And why had they failed? Because they had not sought ends pleasing to God in the attempt to obtain that upon which they could not ask God's blessing. This teaches us a most important lesson, in morals as well as religion. If any question of right arise one has only to ask, Does God wish me to do this?

There need scarcely ever be difficulty in finding a correct answer to that question. The explicit commands of the Holy Scriptures solve a very large proportion of all ethical questions which arise, and the principles laid down in Holy Scripture enable any man of ordinary good sense to frame rules for all recurring emergencies. A superstitious religion is always desiring to have God on its side; but an ethical religion is always studying to be on God's side.

PRAYER.

JAMES is writing very vividly, as though he were face to face with those whom he was reproving. When he intimates that they had sought to obtain by violence what should have been sought in prayer, he seems to hear them exclaim, "Pray! Pray! Why, do we not pray ten times in the day? *we* are not the men to summon to prayer. Call on the heathen." Nay, JAMES would say. You *ask;* you do not *pray*. Your petitions are conceived in sinfulness, and uttered in wickedness. All true prayers made to God, are for something which will enable the supplicant to please and serve God. It is an unhallowed petition which asks for something which I intend to spend on the gratification of my own selfish, sensual, wicked and destroying lusts. It was not for the greater glory of God, and the extension of His kingdom, that the Jews longed for independence and dominion; it was that they might gratify the wicked thirsts of their own corrupt hearts.

Let us be careful of our prayers. They show our hearts to God, and ought to reveal them to ourselves.

IX.
Worldly-mindedness.

CHAPTER IV., 4–17.

REPROACHES.

LOOKING upon the distracted state of Judaism, and seeming to see the ancient people falling away from God, JAMES breaks into strong reproaches.

In the verses 4–6 he thus addresses them: "*Ye adulterers and adulteresses, do ye not know that the friendship of the world is hatred of God? Whosoever, therefore, chooses to be a friend of the world maketh himself an enemy of God. Or, do ye think that the Scripture speaketh emptily? Does the spirit which He has made to dwell in us incline to envy? On the contrary, He giveth a greater grace; for He saith 'God resisteth the proud, but to the humble He giveth grace.'*"

THE RELIGIOUS COVENANT A MARRIAGE.

The spirit of the old prophets seems to have come upon JAMES. The strain in this passage reminds us of the tones in Isaiah and Ezekiel. It is interesting and instructive to observe in the Sacred Scriptures, both of the Old and the New Testament, how the idea of religion is set forth in marriage.

In the New Testament the Apostle represents

marriage as setting forth that mystical union which is between Christ and His Church. And this thought came to him, undoubtedly, from his knowledge of the fact, that the old covenant was regarded as a marriage between Jehovah and His people. Perhaps in this very early and long-cherished connection of thoughts, we may see how adultery has been considered one of the chief crimes; and with that thought, what an appeal it is to any people to be faithful to their religious covenant, by reminding them that the infidelity in this department is as gross and debasing a sin, as infidelity to the marriage relation. It would profit the reader to examine the following passages from the Old Testament Scripture; Ps. 73; Isa. 57; Ez. 23; Hos. 3.

These show us how sacred in the eyes of the Hebrew seers was the bond of union between God and His Church, and how foul they regarded the stain brought upon any soul by any course of thought, or feeling, or conduct, which separated it from its God. That separation was always traced to another love, a love which was illegitimate. We know that the Jews, in the days of JAMES, were greatly given to carnal excesses, and it is possible that in selecting this particular word to indicate spiritual apostasy, he may have also administered a side rebuke to all the carnal modes of life. And the idea is carried forward in what he next says.

He intimates to them that nothing ought to be better known to them than the fact that God has taught that friendship of the world is hatred of God. It was their worldly-mindedness, it was their desire to enjoy this present world, which had led them to envy, to hatred, to wars, to fightings; and so he goes back to the very source of the terrible state of affairs amongst them, and rebukes them, because they were living in violation of their marriage vows to God. He solemnly reminds them that the bride of God could not be the world's bride.

In this passage "the world" is to be understood to be the personification and representation of that which is opposed to God. We must not take morbid views of this subject. So sensible a writer as JAMES could not have meant that those who serve God could not be touched with the beauty of this visible world with its carpeted surface, its brave overhanging sky, its beautiful and constantly varying phenomena, and the great educating power there is in studying the laws of these phenomena. He is not inveighing against æsthetics and science. On the contrary he well knew, as we well know, that love regards with interest the very garments worn by the beloved, and the most devout soul might kiss the visible material as one that loved him might kiss the hem of the garment of a king.

THE LOVE OF GOD AND WORLDLY-MINDEDNESS.

We know, also, for the Scripture teaches us, that they who love God take pleasure in studying His works. Everything of which knowledge can be got by the senses becomes more precious to them, because it is regarded as the work of their adored Lord. But he does point to the fact, that it is possible to become so engaged by the beautiful things of the world, by pomp and display, by gay dress and courtly address, by many things in society that charm the eye, as to have the soul wholly drawn off from God. It is possible, also, so to study, so to become engaged with, the phenomena of the universe and the laws which govern those phenomena, as actually to feel that there is nothing beyond the things which can be reached by the senses, and to worship law as if it were the personal law-giver, and so be lost to God. All such love becomes hatred to God, and as we see throughout human society, the wordly-minded people and materialistic scientists become idolaters, and thus violate the marriage covenant of their souls with God.

It is to be noticed, that the Apostle speaks of this state of mind as being the result of choice. " Whosoever, therefore, *chooses* to be the friend of the world," that is, either allows himself on account of his ungodly inclinations to drift into worldliness, or deliberately makes up his mind for any reason to make the friendship of the world at all costs, does thereby become an enemy of God. He is willing to neglect the indication of God's will; he is willing to violate God's commandment; he is willing to give up all thought of pleasing God, if he can please the world around him.

With all an Israelite's hatred of the heathen, with all a Christian's professions of renunciation, it is possible for one, or the other, or both, to make this dreadful choice.

JAMES'S question must have thrilled his brethren when they first read it, and it may well thrill us and set us to the close examination of our own hearts. Christian people in this day, are surrounded by those who do not fear God and keep His commandments, who are not living "as seeing Him that is invisible," who have no treasures laid up in heaven, who have no plans or purposes which shall extend into an existence beyond the grave. That world is a vain world, that is to say, it is empty of God, empty of faith, empty of hope, and empty of all spiritual life. At best, it has cliques, it has coteries, and it has friendships; it has its fashions, its pleasures and its amusements; but how empty they all are!

WHO IS A "LOVER OF THE WORLD"?

Let us ask ourselves a few questions. Is not he a lover of the world, who makes his choice of friends from worldly men and women, because they are worldly people? Is not he a lover of the world, who is found oftener in places of doubtful or sinful or merely worldly amusement than in the assembly of the saints, in the congregation of the worshippers, in the meeting for prayer? Is not he a lover of the world, who spends more of his income annually in promoting those things which exist simply for society and for this passing world, than he does to promote the spread of the kingdom of God in his own family and among the children of men?

It is not necessary to go into details. Every intelligent person knows the difference between the Church and the world, and every one can settle for himself whether the larger part of his influence goes to the one or to the other. He knows which subordinates the other in his affections. He knows whether in seeking his home, whether in fixing the place of his residence, or in choosing the very church in which he is to worship, he is governed more by the thought of that which will promote the popularity of himself and his family with the people of the world, and give him greater access to all their pleasures and amusements, than by the thought of the spiritual advancement of himself and his children. It is to be remembered, that each one of us belongs either to the friends of the world or to the friends of God.

HOLY SCRIPTURE AGAINST WORLDLY-MINDEDNESS.

Against this worldly-mindedness, which is the father of envy and the grandfather of wars and fightings, JAMES brings the authority of the Holy Scriptures. He appeals to those who had always professed to have reverence for the word of God. He employs a word which was always used to denote the Old Testament — a word occurring more than fifty times in the New Testament, and always applied, and applied only, to those books which the Jews regarded as inspired.

"Can you think lightly of the tenor of the teaching of the Holy Scripture?" is his question. He does not quote any passage from those sacred writings; but he appeals to their reverence for them, and uses the general trend of their teaching to enforce his exhortation to turn from that worldliness which produces envy and all the terrible evils which follow in its train. He might have had in his mind such passages as these: (Job 5: 12), "Wrath killeth and envy slayeth the silly one;" or these words of Solomon (Eccl. 4: 4), "I considered all travail and every right work, that for this a man is envied of his neighbor;" (Prov. 14: 30), "Envy is the rottenness of the bones;" (Prov. 27: 4), "Who is able to stand before envy?"

He may have also had in his mind the cases that had occurred, that were recorded in Sacred Scripture, showing the truth of these sayings. Such is that passage in Isaac's life (Gen. 26) when the envy of the herdmen of Gerar led to a conflict in regard to the well, which thence took the dreadful name Esek, *contention;* or the account (Gen. 30) of Rachel's envy of her sister, which led to such sin and sorrow in the household of Jacob; or the story (Gen. 37) of the envy which the brethren of Joseph had toward him, which brought exile and captivity upon the young brother, years of keenest distress to the old father, and a series of perplexities and mishaps to the family in all its branches. Perhaps the familiar Psalm 106 may have brought the thought of that sin in the camp in the wilderness, when the forefathers "envied Moses, and Aaron the saint of the Lord; when the earth opened and swallowed up Dathan and covered the company of Abiram; when fire was kindled in their company and the flame burned up the wicked." The readers of JAMES might be expected to call to mind the solemn Psalm of Asaph (Ps. 73) in which the devout singer related the painful experience which he had endured, when his "feet were almost gone and his steps had well-nigh slipped, because he was envious of the foolish, when he saw the prosperity of the wicked." He did not need to quote any particular passage from a book which was full of the records of the wickedness of the human heart, and of the direful consequences of that wickedness. Out of the Old Testament take all that refers to this subject and you leave it a blank, almost an "empty" book. But if the subject recurred in the Scriptures only a one-hundredth of the times it does, it ought to be impressive to the heart of a man who had been educated an Israelite.

We may pause to remind ourselves that JAMES appealed to the highest authority in morals existing in his day, namely, the Old Testament Scripture. In our day, Hebrew-Christians and Christian-Hebrews accept the New Testament as of equal authority, while the principle remains that the final appeal amongst men, on any question of morals, must be to the word of the Most High God. What that teaches us to do, it is right to do. What that forbids us to do, it is wrong to do. All other things are indifferent. In questions of ethics, we can do nothing with a man who denies this authority; we can hold no argument with him; we can say nothing to produce conviction, unless our own lives be such as to make the man feel that any teaching which produces such a life must have in it the most powerful ethical energy. We can do nothing with the man who denies the authority of the Holy Scripture, as the word of God, because we have no common standard to which to appeal. It was doubtless the intention of our author to put his assertion in its most effective form by stating it in the shape of a question. If worldliness, enviousness and contentions are not bitter things, the Bible is not worth mentioning; but if the Holy Scripture be the word of God, the most tremendous denunciation from the Supreme Power of the universe is launched against those dreadful sins.

THE HOLY SPIRIT AGAINST WORLDLY-MINDEDNESS.

JAMES brings another argument to bear on this subject. It is founded on the Holy Spirit, which all Christians were supposed to have dwell in them. Was ever envy, with all its dire train of evils, a product of the Holy Spirit? Does ever the Holy Ghost which is in us, secretly and spiritually incline us to worldliness and envy, any more than the same Holy Ghost does in the Bible? Is not "the fruit of the Spirit love, joy, peace, long-suffering, kindness, goodness, meekness, temperance"? Are we not inclined to all these things by the Holy Spirit constantly? And can these things co exist with worldly-mindedness, envy, hatred, malice, and all uncharitableness?

The Holy Spirit, instead of producing these hateful things, so unfavorable to spiritual growth, grants unto us a grace which adorns and enriches our lives, so that it is greater than all the things we can gain by envy and strife; and that we may know that He does give that grace, the Holy Spirit hath said (Prov. 3 : 34) "Surely He scorneth the scorners, but He giveth grace unto the lowly." JAMES was familiar with the Septuagint version of the Old Testament Scriptures, and from it makes this quotation exactly, except that that version has "Lord" instead of "God." But the thought is the same, "God resisteth the proud, but giveth grace to the humble."

GOD IS AGAINST PRIDE.

There is something striking in the prepositions of the Greek version. God puts Himself *against* those who lift themselves *up*. The proud lift themselves up above their own deserts, above their own fellow-men, above their God. On this challenge God puts Himself in battle-array against the proud. We know what will come then, for who can resist God, when once He places His wisdom, His power, His providence against a man? It were well if all the proud would turn themselves to this thought, that pride is a perpetual fight against God, and God is perpetually fighting the proud; that there is nothing in the processes of nature, nothing in the word of God, nothing in the way He has devised for men's salvation which can in the least degree be used to nourish pride; but there is everything to slap pride in the face and spit upon its gewgaws. There is everything in nature, in the word of God, in His providences, in His way of saving men through Jesus Christ, to exalt the humble.

It is impossible for a man to be saved who does not come for salvation with a clear discernment of his real guiltiness and absolute helplessness. But when a man has cast away all pride, and is thoroughly humbled, then God loves to show him favors. There is no peace for the heart, there is no progress for the intellect, there is no salvation of the spirit without humility. The choice given to us all, is between humility and humiliation. It is so in society, and in civil and religious life. Pride comes before destruction in the pursuit of scientific attainments, in acquiring influence over our fellow-men, and in striving to administer ecclesiastical affairs.

He who would learn the secrets of nature, must bow his ear most humbly to her mouth, and never venture proudly to apply his mouth to her ear. No man has added to the real assets of science, who has not studied nature in this spirit. No man has ever largely influenced and led his fellow-men, until they have seen in him a real disposition to be most truly and thoroughly serviceable unto them. The law of the Master is the law of love. He that will be chief among you, must be servant of all.

TRUE CONVERSION—ITS CHARACTERISTICS.

Trusting that his words had made an impression upon his brethren, JAMES proceeds to instruct them in the characteristics of true conversion.

"*Be subject, therefore, unto God. Resist the devil, and he will flee from you. Draw nigh to God, and He will draw nigh to you. Cleanse your hands, ye sinners; and purify your hearts, ye double-souled. Be greatly afflicted and mourn and wish to weep: let your laughter be turned into mourning and your joy into sadness. Humble yourselves in the presence of the Lord, and He will lift you up."*

SUBMISSION TO GOD.

The first thing necessary for a thorough, hearty change in the whole moral life of a man, is to submit himself to God. There are no sanctions of morality to an atheist. He that does not believe in a personal God cannot be a moral man. It is not said that he will not do many things which are right, many things which the moral men around him do; it is not said that he may not even find what he calls "data of ethics," and formulate some sort of system, either from utilitarianism, which finds that right to do which it is *profitable* to do, or from hedonism, which finds that to be right which administers to the personal *pleasure*.

NO MORALITY POSSIBLE TO ATHEISM.

But on whatever ground he may put his intellectual system, there is nothing to bind him. Supposing a man had precisely the data of ethics known to the mind of God, and had formulated precisely the system which stands in the mind of God, and suppose he even endeavored to conform his life steadily to this system, he might still be an immoral man. He would be if he had no sanction to his system. The *data* and the *system* are inoperative without a *sanction*, and there seems to be no conceivable sanction of morality, which does not have reference to a person of paramount moral authority; and a person of paramount moral authority is a synonyme for God.

One easily perceives that, supposing it were known what course of conduct would bring the greatest good to the greatest number, the question still remains unanswered, why is any man bound to bring the greatest good to the greatest number? What obligation is he under to the greatest number? What has the greatest number ever done for him? How does a favor create an obligation? Why is it not better to do that which is more profitable to a man's self than that which is more profitable to all mankind, supposing that there could be two entirely diverse courses thus described?

Again, why should a man pursue that course of conduct which brings the greatest pleasure to himself? What binds him to such a course if he choose to take another which brings less pleasure to himself? Whatever puts on the semblance of an ethical idea, which does not have in itself a clear conception of a paramount personality who must be obeyed, is no ethical idea at all. The essence of the ethical idea is obedience to another, to One who is superior to all and has authority over all.

WHO IS A MORAL MAN?

A moral person is one who has a God whom he feels he ought to obey, who consequently feels that that God has conveyed to him some instruction which he can understand and must obey, who, believing these two things, does obey the injunctions of his God, and simply and solely because they are divine injunctions.

Wherefore, the beginning of all morality, and of all religion, is the perfect subjection of the human to the divine, of the man to his God. He could not be a moral personality himself if he could not rebel against that God, and there would be no moral element in any cultivated thought, feeling, or action unless that culture were undertaken of choice on the part of the man. In other words, if God did compel a man to do certain things, keep His commandments for instance, there would be no morality in a life thus poured by the hand of God like molten lead into the moulds God has made. Submit *yourselves* assumes, therefore, the personal freedom of those addressed, and their capability of cherishing ethical thoughts and feelings, and of performing ethical acts. The added phrase, "to God," makes the submission moral.

There can come no peace to any man who struggles against God. There will always be trouble in his moral nature. Peace comes with harmony, and harmony with accord, and accord with the rule of the superior over the inferior and the submission of the inferior to the superior. Wherefore, submission to God is the beginning of all good living. It will involve breaking with the world, denying the supremacy of society, throwing off the yoke of Mammon, and drawing out the whole life by the rule of God.

WHAT IS A DEVIL?

A devil is whatever strives to draw us away from that allegiance to God. *The* devil is the prince of the power of the air; the exerter of an influence as impalpable and as invisible as the air, and yet as pervasive; what we sometimes call "the spirit of the age." Him we ought to resist. It is a degrading superstition which makes men feel, if they do not exactly believe it, that the devil is omnipotent. In these brief apophthegms, JAMES sets forth picturesquely the spiritual dynamics in the spiritual world. As cunning in any individual produces cowardice, so with all his subtlety and strength the devil is a coward. Any resolute child can put him to flight. All one needs is to *resist* the devil. The strongest and loftiest saint will be tempted, but the youngest and feeblest child need not yield to temptation. The wrong is not in being tempted, but in not resisting. If men who are drunken or licentious, would set even their enfeebled moral wills resolutely to never tasting a drop of that which intoxicates, to never looking upon that which tempts; if they would thoroughly believe and perpetually act upon this brief saying of JAMES, as embodying an inflexible principle in the spiritual world, "Resist the devil, and he will flee from you," how triumphant would become lives which now succumb to evil. But it is submission to God which gives power to resist the devil.

WHY MEN DO NOT SUBMIT TO GOD.

One reason why men do not submit to God is, that He is in their imagination something afar off, a distant, dim ideal, instead of a real personality very close to them. God is near every one of us. In Him we live and move and have our being. But who has not learned that there may be personal nearness co-existing with moral and spiritual distance? How often husband and wife have eaten every meal at the same table, and slept together every night in the same bed, with their affections as far from each other as could be those of any two total strangers. How often between husband and wife have been put all the lands and the seas of a hemisphere, while every waking hour of the day, and often in dreams, they were near each other.

"So near and yet so far" is an oft-quoted expression, to signify physical contiguity existing at the same moment with spiritual distance. "So far and yet so near" is the expression of an experience very common to those who love the Lord. We cannot draw nearer to Him who is everywhere present, so far as locality is concerned, but we can draw near in heart. Jehovah was as near to the people on the plain as He was to Moses on the Mount; and Moses on the Mount with God, would have been no nearer God if the heart of Moses had been down in the plain with the golden calf.

DRAWING NIGH TO GOD.

This drawing nigh to God is the expression of a specific operation of the general law of attraction in the spiritual world. In the physical world there is no volition; in the spiritual world there is. You may will to lessen the attraction which some things have upon you, and you may will to increase the power of the attraction of others. What is implied in drawing near to God, seems to involve a cultivation of reverence for Him. That reverence presupposes a belief in His existence, in the greatness of His character, and in the claims which He has upon our souls.

All men who have had any spiritual experience, know that it is possible to increase this reverence for the great God. The word, also, is as old as the Old Testament Scripture. It means an act of dedication to God. We go forward to Him. The use of all spiritual sanctuaries is, that by going to the holy places, a man may indicate, and at the same time increase, the approaches which he makes reverentially in his spirit to God.

It implies also spiritual intimacy with God, and increasing knowledge of His character, of His ways, of His will toward the children of men. It implies an alertness of the intellect, and of the heart, toward God's truths and God's love, which may be represented by a little child's quick ear for the least call of its mother's voice. It will be shown by a man' feelings everywhere for God, that haply he may find Him nigh, and by his intense desire to know, as the smitten Saul of Tarsus did, what the Lord would have him do.

We are perpetually meeting in society with two classes of men, both of whom are seeking peace and happiness. One put God far away; when they remember God, they are troubled. They never open the Bible, they never kneel in prayer, they never assemble themselves with the saints. They go as far as they can from everything which reminds them of the divine sovereignty, hoping, by forgetfulness of God, to lose also a sense of their own danger. There are other men, who watch every sign that stirs in the heavens above, and in the earth beneath, that if possible they may detect some signal of the hand of God, and find some divine finger pointing in the way of right; and they are always rewarded.

ILLUSTRATED BY THE CASE OF ABRAHAM.

The story is told (Genesis 18) of the patriarch Abraham's sitting in the tent door, in the heat of the day, on the plains of Mamre. He lifted up his eyes and saw three men. A man who was always looking for God would hail any new appearance, as probably some little larger opening in the veil which hangs before our natural sense and excludes the spiritual world. And so it is said that Abraham ran to meet them, and bowed himself toward the ground. If he had been under the influence of an evil superstition, or if he had been a man who feared to know more of God, he would have run, through the back of his tent, out into the plain and away from God, and have missed that blessed interview which changed his whole life and became a benediction to the world.

THE CASE OF MOSES.

If, also, Moses, while keeping the flock of Jethro, his father-in-law, in the backside of the desert (Exodus 3) had turned away in fright from the flaming bush, another interview would have been avoided, an interview which has changed the history of the world. This instance affords, also, an illustration of the results to which men are led who are devoutly scientific. He had stept aside to see *why* the bush was not burned. He was sure God was doing something there, and he wished to see what it was, when God, out of the burning bush, called his name. If he had been foolishly or sinfully superstitious, he would have fled in dismay down the crags of Horeb. Instead of this, when he heard his name called, he answered, "Here am I." Here the steps of the right-minded man are shown. First, he studies what God is doing; then he hears what God is saying, and when the call is made to him, he gives that high ethical answer, "Here am I." There was no danger that he should become too intimate with God; there is no danger that any of us shall. God taught him where to stop. A man who wishes to be a really true man will keep on going when God starts him, and never cease till God halts him; when halted, he will stay there forever, or until God command him to move.

THE CASE OF ISAIAH.

A similar experience came to Isaiah, in the year that King Uzziah died, when he saw the Lord sitting upon a throne, high and lifted up, His train filling the temple, surrounded by the seraphim, who cried to one another, and said, "Holy, holy, holy, is the Lord of Hosts, and the whole earth is full of His glory," until the posts of the door moved at the voice of them that cried. But he did not fly; he simply humbled himself unto God, and a live coal was taken by the hands of a seraph, and laid on his lips, till his iniquity was taken away and his sin purged (Isa. 6).

Now how shall *we* draw near to God? Where is God? God is in Christ (2 Cor. 5:19). The nearer I can get to this blessed personality, in my understanding of His true character, in my imbibing of His spirit, in my intimate co-operation with His plans for human advancement, I shall be drawing nearer to God. There are the Holy Scriptures; they have become to the modern Church what the pavilion of Jehovah was to His ancient people; namely, a pillar of cloud by day and of light by night. I draw near, therefore, unto God when I bring myself close to all the promises God hath made to me in the Sacred Scriptures; and I draw near to God when I give my affectionate belief to all the doctrines which are taught in the Sacred Scriptures. The one is my cloud to protect me from evil while engaged in the work of the day, and the other is my light to brighten me in the night of my trouble. "The mind of the Spirit is the word of God;" the heart of Jesus is the word of God; the truth of the Father is the word of God. As I bring my intellect, my heart, and my life, closer and closer to the blessed Book, I am drawing nigher and nigher to God.

The law of attraction prevails here also, and brings from the pen of JAMES the blessed assurance that, "if we draw near to God, He will draw near to us"; and He Himself hath revealed to us, in all the record the Bible gives of His intercourse with His saints, how one step of theirs toward God is helped by the rapid approach of God unto them. Nowhere in Scripture is this more touchingly shown than in the many-sided story of the return of the Prodigal Son. Ruined, humiliated, degraded, and dejected, he slowly comes toward his father's house. He knows how good his father is; but knows, also, how vile he is himself. When the father sees him, he does not re-enter his house and shut the portals of his mansion against his boy. He does not go down the avenue with slow, majestic steps, not moving one foot until his son has moved two; but on the wings of loving mercifulness and fatherly affection, he rushes to his son. And while that son does not dare to look him straight in the eyes, much less to put his soiled hands on the sacred person of his father, the father wraps his son in the arms of his love, and covers him with the caresses of his affection. So, the man who draws near to God, God draws with great rapidity toward Himself.

CLEANSED HANDS.

"Cleanse the hands, ye sinners." In Scripture language this phrase is always used to mean the putting away of evil deeds. As the feet represent the course which a man takes, and show the direction of his life, the hands are always known as the instruments for doing. The cleansing of the hands, therefore, signifies the putting away of evil deeds. One must cease to do evil before one can learn to do well. The very order in which JAMES puts the ideas here, is the order of the Old Testament Scripture. Those who ascend into the hill of the Lord are those who have clean hands and a pure heart (Ps. 24 : 4). And David said, "I will wash my hands in innocency; *so* will I compass Thine altar, O Lord." But exterior reformation is of but little help to a man; the work must go deeper; his heart must be cleansed. If all the badness of a past life could be taken and cast into the midst of the sea, there is still the corrupt heart, which will reproduce all the evil of a life. The fruit of the tree will be of the nature of the tree, and it is intimated that while the sin of the life comes from wicked activity, the sin of the heart comes from double-mindedness. There must be no vacillation. The love of the world must be given up thoroughly; there is no sanctification till all affections are given to God. The want of purity of heart is evidently produced by double-mindedness. None can come to these experiences who are not afflicted, who do not afflict themselves, whose grief is not really deep, the remembrance of whose sins does not bow them down to the very ground.

When conviction for a man's sin takes hold of him, it is so natural that he should attempt to comfort himself before getting rid of his sins; and it is because there is some sort of temporary comfort, at least some forgetfulness, to be found by engaging in other things, that men do not go immediately with penitence and faith to God, for absolution and for cleansing. A very striking instance of this is recorded in Isaiah (22 : 12), "And in that day did the Lord God of Hosts call to weeping, and to mourning, and to baldness, and to girding with sackcloth. And behold, joy and gladness, selling oxen and killing sheep, eating flesh and drinking wine. Let us eat and drink, for to-morrow we shall die." JAMES warns us against this fatal fallacy, this tremendous mistake of endeavoring to narcotize our convictions by sinful pleasures. When, under the preaching of the Gospel, our souls are struck with the arrows of conviction for our sins, let us not go out and attempt to drown those disturbing convictions in wine, and wear away those salutary distresses in wassail. That is what was done in the days of Isaiah. God knew what was necessary for the souls of His people; but instead of obeying Him, they endeavored to put out of their minds the call of God which they were disobeying, and so they were destroyed.

If some one could have come upon their feasts, and turned their laughter into mourning and their joy into sadness, they might have been saved. How instable a thing is laughter after all. There is a time to laugh and a sense of humor is wholesome; but when one comes to think carefully over his past life and recall his seasons of hilarity, how little they appear to have contributed to the upbuilding of his character. Jokes and witticisms which gave us our laughter have made almost no permanent impression upon our character or destiny.

Nothing can be a greater mistake than to suppose that religious humility is at all akin to intellectual or spiritual degradation. He that humbles himself before God, need humble himself before no man. It is impossible to think of the archangel in heaven as a degraded being or the cherubim and seraphim as degraded beings, because they all veil their faces with their wings and bow before the Father of eternity, as He sits on the supreme throne of the universe, and cry to Him, "Holy, holy, holy, Lord God Almighty; heaven and earth are full of the majesty of Thy glory." That leaves no place for archangelic or seraphic or cherubic glory, and none of those lofty beings desire any glory that is apart from that of God.

EVIL SPEAKING.

In the next verses (11, 12), JAMES warns his brethren against evil speaking.

"Do n t speak one against another, brethren. He who speaketh against his brother and condemneth his brother, speaketh against the law and condemneth the law. But if thou condemnest the law, thou art not a doer of the law, but a judge. One there is, a Law-giver able to save and to destroy. Thou, who art thou, that judgest another?"

There are few more evident and more painful indications of the corruption of our nature than the general tendency to detraction. In all ages of the world, men seem to be more able to display their wit and their other intellectual resources in calumny than in eulogy. When a man comes to you, and says, "I heard a man speak about you yesterday," you immediately take it for granted that that man said something *against* you. It is painful to note that the tendency of human nature is exactly adverse to a common-sense principle, which is assumed in all Christian courts of law, in criminal cases, namely, that a man must be presumed to be innocent until he be proved to be guilty. In Christian society, the mode of procedure is that in Turkish courts, namely, the assumption that the defendant is guilty, rolling upon him the necessity of establishing his innocence. Few things can be conceived more hurtful than this. Moreover, in most instances of detraction, the person is absent, and so ordinarily has not an opportunity of even attempting the gravely difficult task of establishing his innocence.

SPIRIT OF CONTRADICTION.

Akin to this is the spirit of contradiction, which leads so many people to take it for granted that whatever opinion or sentiment has originated with another must therefore be wrong. These two courses of conduct lead to very many of the ills of society. Detraction is hurtful every way. It hurts the detractor by increasing the power of the habit of evil-speaking. It injures the listener by increasing the pessimistic tendencies of his own heart and his want of confidence in human nature. It injures the absent by a denial of his right of self-defence.

EVIL HEARING.

Many of the injurious effects of evil-speaking might be avoided if men could be made to feel the sin of *evil-hearing*. To listen to the calumny is only a less sin than to utter it. If every Christian man determined that he would immediately rise and leave the room the very moment any one began to speak evil of the absent, the rebuke would go far to silence the voice of the detractor. It is because we love to hear evil of our neighbor that his neighbor loves to speak evil of him. He sees it gives us pleasure, and the conversationalist has his delight in the enjoyment which he sees he imparts to his listener.

THE MOSAIC LAW.

JAMES strengthens his appeal to his brethren by calling their attention to *the law*—which here may mean either the Mosaic law by itself, or, the Mosaic law of right completed by the Christian law of love. If it refer alone to the former, this is the last time that the law of Moses is mentioned in the Sacred Scriptures. That law has very severe denunciations of calumny, slander and other evil-speaking; so that he who is guilty of it, condemns the Mosaic law. If the latter, then Christians are all the more guilty when they indulge in evil-speaking, because, while the law came by Moses, grace and truth came by Jesus Christ. Those to whom JAMES wrote, prided themselves on their zeal for the law; "but," says he, "habitual evil-speaking is a course of conduct which denies that the law which forbids it is a good law." An evil-speaker says, by his course of conduct, either that Moses and Christ were wrong in their judgment, or that neither has any authority over the detractor's conscience. It is to be noticed here, that the phrases "he that speaketh against his brother" and "condemneth his brother," do not indicate a solitary performance of the act, but do point to the habit of evil-speaking. But we must remind ourselves, how difficult it is to speak evil of a neighbor occasionally without falling into the dreadful habit.

ONE LAWGIVER.

He furthermore strengthens his appeal to them by calling their attention to that One who is the supreme law-giver; and the words which he uses, show that he certainly means Jesus the Christ as the law-giver, and His Gospel as the law, even if Moses be included. Christ is the one law-giver to His Church, and no man has a right to make a law for believers which Christ Himself has not distinctly made. So when these worldly-minded, envious and calumniating Hebrew-Christians undertook to lay down laws for the guidance of their brethren, and undertook to judge and condemn their brethren by their own standard, they were assuming the tremendous responsibility which belongs to Jehovah's Christ.

No men and no body of men who have not the ability to enforce laws are empowered to make laws. Now there is only one in the universe who is able to save and to destroy a man's spirit. No private Christian can do it; no ecclesiastic, high or low, can do it; no Church councils have power to make any law to bind any conscience, because none of these can either lift a soul to heaven or cast it down to hell. There is One Law-giver and One Judge and One Executive in the universe, and that is the Lord. What a terrible thing it is for any man to put himself in the place of the One who was enthroned on Sinai as the world's moral law-giver, and was enthroned on Golgotha as the world's spiritual Savior, and shall be enthroned on the judgment-seat on the last day as the universal Judge.

THE RESTLESS SPIRIT.

In the time of the writer of this epistle, those Hebrews who had become Christians were much infected with the restless spirit of those who had continued as Israelites of the strictest set, and with them were scattered abroad, wandering about amongst all peoples; and because they had no home, and were not long enough settled for agricultural pursuits, their passion and their skill for trading grew and carried them everywhere. They were betrayed into a presumptuous confidence that all things would continue as they were. This led them into forming plans of the future without reference to God; and to this fault JAMES calls their attention (4, 13-16):

"*Here, now, ye who are accustomed to say, 'To-day and to-morrow, and we shall journey to this or that city, and work there a year, and traffic, and get gain;' ye, who do not know aught of to-morrow. (Why, what kind of thing is your life? Why, a vapor it is, which for a little time is in sight, but even then is vanishing.) Instead of your saying, 'If the Lord will, we shall both live and do this or that.' But now you rejoice in your boastings. All such rejoicing is evil."*

The conditions of the times were such that ordinarily the Jewish trader took the goods that were cheap in one place, and carried them to another, where they were in more demand, and consequently brought a higher price; and so he would go from place to place, buying in one and selling in another, all the while accompanying his commodities. This involved his stopping a short time in each place visited, that he might complete his mercantile transaction. Thus he would move to Damascus, Antioch, Alexandria, Smyrna, Corinth, wherever he could buy at the smallest and sell at the largest price.

SELF-CONFIDENCE.

It is easy to see how such a merchant would glide into self-confidence, and forget to calculate for casualties in making schedules of journeyings for himself; saying, "I will start to-day, or, if that be not convenient, I will start to-morrow, and go first to this city, and then to that; and when I reach the designated place, I will enter upon selling and buying of merchandise; in doing which my former experience justifies me in believing that I shall increase my estate." Such entire self-confidence was injurious to that state of mind a Christian should maintain, in which he would lean wholly upon God; daily praying, "Thy will be done," and every day striving to fulfil his own prayer, as much as in him lay, by doing the will of God.

JAMES recalls them from their folly by the sharp question, "What kind of a thing is your life?" Is it like the Appian Way, a road laid on the solid ground, which you can measure mile by mile, which you can pass over to-day and come back twenty years from this and find the same road still there? No; human life is never such a thing as that. On the contrary, it is like a vapor, a vapor which may rise into the air, and spread itself out largely, and become splendid with the rays of the rising or setting sun; but still it is a vapor; it does not continue for two successive minutes in the same form. It is a thing which is visible to the eye; but while one is looking upon it, it is in the very moment of vanishing. To rely upon that as a solid thing, is to build castles in the air. The temper of mind and the mode of speech which befit a Christian are in the saying, "If the Lord will, we shall both live and do the things which we propose."

THE "DEO VOLENTE."

We are not to understand that every time a Christian man speaks of his projects he is to bring in a

Deo volente phrase. If that were done every time an intention were announced it is obvious that it would soon make conversation ridiculous, if any attention were paid to it; if the words were spoken without attention, they would degenerate into cant, that is, the use of words which we had emptied of their meaning, and would also savor of profanity, because it would be taking the name of God in vain.

But on the other hand, if there be not formed in our spirits the habit of continual reference to the will of God, and continual reliance upon His personal protection and providence, there will come into the spirit a boasting which will be neither beautiful nor profitable. One thing is certain, we must always take God into the calculation; we must always have reference to His will; we shall thus secure for ourselves the divine guidance, for the promise is that if in all our ways we acknowledge the Lord, He will direct our paths (Prov. 3:6); and then the disappointments of life will not smite us with such tremendous force. We are not principals, we are agents. We are doing the work of God under the direction of God. If our work miscarry, we can refer what seems the mishap to God, and thus change it into what may be the very best thing for us and for all men.

The moral lessons of this admonition are as timely and as binding in our days as in the days in which it was written, and perhaps more so. There never has been an age in which there was so much traveling as in ours. More persons went from one place to another last year than in any other year since the world began. There were more journeys undertaken last year than ever before. It is an age of movement; the invention of modes of motion is the passion of our times. The extension of railways on the planet during the past decade has been something enormous. Never did so many people run to and fro as are so running now.

The same is true of trade. More people are shipping and receiving goods than ever before. There was a time when the spirit of the feudal system made trade below the dignity of persons of what was called "quality." In modern times, in the Southern States of our country, the same spirit prevailed before the Civil War; so that no lady ever engaged in any other work than housewifery, no lady would even sell a poem or a story for money. But almost every man trades in England and in the South to-day. Men are keeping shop whose grandfathers would have considered it more disgrace to have bought and sold than to have committed almost any kind of sin, men whose fathers could boast that for five hundred years not a single ancestor had ever made a shilling by trade. To-day women, with noble blood in their veins, are opening shops in London for millinery and other dry goods. Business is done on a larger scale than ever before; bargains are made to amounts that exceed the worth of principalities. Where men used to buy, as it were, handfuls of sand, men are to-day buying and selling great mountain ranges. If ever there were a time in which the injunction of JAMES should be heeded, this is the time.

Into every syndicate God should be taken as a partner. Every journey should be undertaken under His direction. All success should be ascribed to Him, not necessarily openly and by word of mouth, certainly never ostentatiously, but as certainly, always really and devoutly. Otherwise our boastings will be evil, and will confirm us in that self-confidence which by and by will be our destruction.

X.

The Sin of Uselessness.

CHAPTER IV., 17.

A PRINCIPLE OF VARIED APPLICATION.

WE can imagine that, after delivering all these precepts, JAMES could fancy hearing his brethren reply, "Oh, all this is very true; we have read it in the Scriptures." And that leads him to utter in one sentence a principle of varied application, and of a very wide-spread importance:

"Therefore, to him that knoweth to do good, and doeth it not, to him it is sin."

Perhaps few of us have considered what multitudes there are everywhere who rely upon their knowledge of the truth, while that knowledge is absolutely inoperative. They never "do." They hear, but do not put into practice. They read, but they do not allow it to regulate their lives. What most men in Christendom need to-day is not so much more instruction in morals as a greater stimulation of conscience. It is a tremendous responsibility, which men assume, to hear three or four religious discourses a week, while they are allowing no portion of the truth to have any influence on their practical lives. It is a sin to hold back in my intellect a truth which I ought to allow to affect my emotions and to regulate my intercourse with my fellow-men.

SINS OF "COMMISSION" AND "OMISSION."

This is so important a subject that it must be dwelt upon. How common is the classification of sins into those of commission and of omission; and how common is the mistake that the former are the more hurtful. Even in our prayers we ask pardon for "our sins of commission" and "our sins of omission," and the tones of our voice show that the latter are put apart, as in a parenthesis, and are considered not at all heinous. We must arouse ourselves to the truth that sins of omission may be much worse than the worst sins of commission, as they are called. These latter, such as murder and adultery, may be committed in the heat of passion, and may break out perhaps only once in a man's life; his character may then be like a house which has been smitten by a storm-blast, having a chimney knocked down, or the corner of the roof torn off; but sins of omission are like a dry rot which reduces the whole edifice to such a state that at any moment it may drop into a heap of dust.

In studying this subject we may consider the classification of the commandments in the moral law into those which enjoin and those which forbid; those which say "Thou shalt," and those which say "Thou shalt not." And we are thinking, and talking, and acting as if the violation of the latter were all the sins worth accounting. For instance, we never for a moment doubt that to violate the commandment "Thou shalt not steal," or the commandment "Thou shalt not kill," or the commandment "Thou shalt not commit adultery," is a sin. But who charges his conscience equally with the violation of the commandment "Remember that thou keep holy the Sabbath Day," or "Honor thy father and thy mother"? And so, if a man has observed every one of the Ten Commandments which has the word *not* in it, and is suddenly arrested as a sinner, he turns upon his accuser with the surprised inquiry, "Why, what have I done?" and does not perceive that that very question points to the ground of his condemnation. Yes, that is a much more important question than the other, "What have I *not* done?" It is *the* question that shall be urged upon the conscience at the final judgment, "What *hast* thou done?"

We must remind ourselves that sin consists not only in disregarding the prohibitions, but also in failing to come up to the requirements, of the positive injunctions of the law of God. We, whose lives have always been perfectly honest as touching the property of other people, are to remember that the same authority which binds us to honesty in the Fourth Commandment, equally binds us to beneficence in the commandment

"Do good unto all men." Now, if I have had an opportunity to do good and have not done it, I am just as certainly a sinner as if I had had an opportunity to abstract my neighbor's property and had stolen it.

THE PROCESS OF DESCENT.

Let us trace the history of the fall. The account given us in Holy Scripture shows that man was first led away from righteousness and then led into sin. The history of that one transaction is an epitome of the lives of good people in all ages, who have fallen away. Sins of omission precede sins of commission, and as invariably, sins of commission succeed sins of omission. The man that neglects the study of the Sacred Scriptures and the cultivation of a prayerful spirit in private, is a man whose life comes to be stained with violations of those commandments which forbid certain courses of conduct.

THE PROCESS OF ASCENT.

So when a man is converted he retraces these steps. He first "ceases to do evil" and then "learns to do well." Such also is the effect of the atonement, which we have through our Lord Jesus Christ. It does these two things in their order: first, it secures a man his pardon; and then it sets him upon paths of usefulness. Mere harmlessness may be possible for inanimate things. A stone, or the stump of a tree on the inaccessible height of a mountain may do no harm to anybody. But how is it possible that any living thing should maintain that position in the universe? More especially, how is it possible that a sentient being, with a conscience and such other activities as belong to man as man, could remain in the neutral position of a stock or a stone? Every human being is either doing good or doing evil every day of his life.

At the point of time when a soul receives the pardon of his sins, he enters on a new spiritual departure. From that moment it is impossible that he shall lead a life of mere uselessness. If he could, one day in such a state would be a day of sin.

Is there anything which stands out more distinctly in the teachings of our Lord Jesus Christ than the doctrine of the sin of not doing good? Is there anything upon which, by precept and by picturesque illustration in parable, He laid more and more emphasis than upon the teaching that a man must not only be harmless, but that he must *be* good and *do* good?

THE ACTED PARABLE.

One of the most impressive of the teachings of Jesus is an unspoken parable taught by one of His most impressive acts. One morning He saw a fig-tree in the road. The tree had leaves, and therefore, according to its nature, should have had fruit. Jesus cursed it; it was the only thing He cursed in all His wonderful career; and the tree withered. What was there in this tree which brought such a doom? Was the fig-tree a bad growth amongst the trees? On the contrary, the tree itself, when it bore fruit, gave that which is sweet to the taste and nourishing to the body. Was the tree doing any harm? Was it exuding poison, which might fall like the distillation of the upas tree on the eyes of the sleeper below, or be destructive to the birds and insects that alighted amid its leaves? Was it even keeping other plants from growing? Is there the slightest intimation that there was anything harmful in the existence of the tree by the road-side? Not the slightest. But there is a fearful lesson of the wrong of unfruitfulness, which, in the case of this tree, was aggravated by the additional sin of pretence. A fig-tree that has not figs has no right to leaves. There is a subsidiary lesson here: one of the dangers of unfruitfulness is the temptation which it affords to hypocrisy. So wide-spread is the lesson that all religious people should lead lives of beneficence. When a man stands in the Church and does no good, he is very liable to put on the pretence of usefulness, as the tree did.

THE DESTRUCTIVE NAPKIN.

There is the well-known parable of Jesus (Matthew 25) of the talents which a lord had committed to his servants.

He to whom had been committed five, doubled them; he who had two, doubled them; and the latter received precisely the commendation which was given to the former; showing that it is not the amount in the result, but it is the activity in the life, which the Lord approves. There was a third servant to whom one talent had been committed. When the lord came to take account of his servants, the man with the one talent came forward with it, and returned it precisely as he had received it. There was not the slightest portion lost. In weight and value it was exactly as it was when months or years ago his lord had put it in his hand. He had not spent any portion of his lord's money upon his desires or his needs. No selfishness had been sufficient to induce him to run away with his lord's money. No companionship had induced him, by any social seduction, to waste any of his lord's money in riotous living. He had not been careless of his talent, allowing others to take away his lord's money. He had preserved it by carefully wrapping it in a napkin and putting it where no thief could break in. He had guarded it vigilantly and preserved the knowledge of the hiding-place. He considered himself a brilliant example of a harmless man. And he was. When the day of account came, he appeared promptly and, with an air of great self-satisfaction, more so apparently than either of his fellow-servants, he cheerfully said to his lord, " There, take—that is thine."

He believed his lord to be a severe master, and yet

he felt that if, after long absence, upon his return, his master should find exactly the talent which the servant returned all unhurt, there could be no fault found. And yet how tremendous were the words of the master in reproof of his servant! What was his fault? Nothing but this: that he had had an opportunity to increase something committed to his care, and he had neglected to make such improvement. And yet he fell under the condemnation of such a sentence as this from the lips of his master: " Take therefore the talent from him and give it unto him which has ten talents; for unto every one that hath shall be given, and he shall have abundance, but from him that hath not, shall be taken away even that which he hath; and cast ye the unprofitable servant into outer darkness. There shall be weeping and gnashing of teeth."

SIN IN PURPLE.

That outer darkness reappears in the parable of the rich man and Lazarus (Luke 16). Whatever opinion may be held as to whether the conclusion of the story lay in this world or in the world to come, there can be no difficulty as to this: that the intention is to present in the most vivid language which Jesus could employ the dread sinfulness of a useless life, and the horror with which it is regarded by the Heavenly Father. What was the character of this rich man? Did he fail to read the Holy Scriptures? Did he fail to attend upon public service? Did he ever wrong any man of his money, or rob any woman of her virtue? Was he a thief, a liar, a murderer? What had he done; what against God, what against man? So far as the record goes, absolutely nothing. His circumstances put him beyond the temptations which lead to the commission of many sins. He was rich; he had abundance; he did not have to steal his bread in order to preserve his life. He not only did no harm, but he did not stand in the way of other people's doing good. He did not prevent his servants from shaking out broken dainties and tidbits from the table-cloths which served at his own meals. When he passed out to his business or his pleasure and saw a loathsome pauper at his door, he did not kick him for being there, he did not even order his servants to remove him. But day by day this wretched beggar lay and had some food, enough indeed to sustain his life, for a long time, from the table of this rich man. What had he done? Nothing, absolutely nothing, but this: he had had opportunity to be good to another, and had simply failed to do it. Yet when he died, he was in torments, such torments that led him to cry for a drop of water to cool his tongue. If human language can fix upon the memory by sentences more picturesque than these *the sinfulness of not doing good*, who will devise the song, or the sermon, or the story, more impressive than this parable of Jesus?

THE LAST JUDGMENT.

If any one should think for a moment that this is a solitary case, let him read the twenty-fifth chapter of the Gospel according to Matthew, and follow up this and the parable of the talents with the account which Jesus gives of the general judgment; when, before the throne of the glory of the Great Judge, shall be gathered all nations, and the King shall invite some into the Kingdom prepared for them, on the ground that their faith had been operative, and had led them to feed the hungry and give drink to the thirsty, and hospitality to the stranger, and clothes to the naked, and visits to the sick, and attention to the prisoner. Then, when these have been gathered into the Kingdom, what shall become of all the others? The Judge is represented as saying to them, "Depart from Me, ye cursed, into everlasting fire prepared for the devil and his angels." He curses them; He pronounces their doom. No fire was ever prepared for human beings, but there has been a fire prepared for the devil and his emissaries, and men may prepare themselves for the torture which that fire can inflict.

According to the opinion of Him who knows the secrets of all hearts, how does one prepare one's self for such a doom as that? By Sabbath-breaking, lying, theft, robbery, adultery, murder? Most surely these sins will make a man a fit companion for the devil and his staff. The Judge, however, says nothing of these so obvious things, but He does point to what as inevitably brings a man into fitness for companionship with the devil, namely, a life barren of all good. From this fearful rehearsal of the judgment scene by the Lord Jesus, the more fearful because it is uttered in such a quiet tone, we learn that one does not have to commit every capital offence in the law. Unfruitfulness, uselessness, the absence of beneficence—this will certainly bring a man to this dreadful doom. All one has to do is to live in a world where there is hunger and thirst and loneliness and nakedness and sickness and imprisonment, and not minister food and drink and companionship and clothing and visitation, to the least of one of Christ's brethren, that is, to the least of human beings, for Jesus Christ, the Son of Man, is the brother of all men.

Those whom He says He will be compelled to condemn at the last judgment, will not simply be those who mistreated Him; not some who had taken away the food He may have had in his hand, or dashed the cup of water from His lips when He was fevered, or stripped His raiment from Him, or cast Him into prison; not simply those who spat upon His face, who lashed Him on the bare back, who pressed the thorn-crown into His holy brow, who nailed Him to the accursed cross; but with them shall go all those who, *knowing to do good, do it not.*

Who shall be able to read these teachings of our Lord, and study His example, and remember that His human career is epitomized in the statement " He went about doing good"; who shall study the career of His Apostles, and see what prodigiously fortifying power there was in their faith, which not only saved them, but sent them out to save others ; and shall not have impressed upon himself the great truth, that every hour of human life which is not spent in useful employment is an hour of sin ? If JAMES had written no other sentence, this last verse of his fourth chapter is enough to place him in the foremost ranks of all ethical teachers and win him an immortality of fame.

COMMON SENSE APPLIES THE PRINCIPLE.

In an age of such multifarious modes of intercommunication as our own time, it is easy to perceive how we all can learn modes of doing good much more rapidly than we can increase our ability to do good. The precept of JAMES must be read, therefore, in the light of common sense. The writer of these pages, as well perhaps as the reader, knows a thousand ways in which he can do good, where he has the ability to employ only five of them. An important question then arises as to the extent of our responsibility. That is plainly limited by our ability. No man can be held to answer for not doing what he cannot do. Then, when it is settled that all our ability to do good must be employed, the selection has to be made from the many and multiform methods of usefulness which present themselves to our attention.

THE NEAREST FIRST.

Duty is created by obligation. Obligation is the result of many factors. Nearness is one of these. My first obligation is to myself; I know how to do good to myself. Here is a personality to deal with from whom I am never absent. No mother, nor wife, nor child, can be as near me as myself. That very constancy of contiguity creates an obligation. The person who is to be the first object of my religious care is myself. There can be no obligation which precedes that which binds me to myself. Doing good to any human being is the treatment of him in such a manner as will tend to make him good. Being good means serving God. Now, each man must turn upon himself, and do all he can by preserving the health and nursing the powers of his body, cultivating the faculties of his intellect, purifying his emotions, and stimulating his spirit. If he knows any course of hygiene, or education, or devout exercise needed to accomplish these things, and he neglects it, he is so far forth a sinner. His neighbor does not have precedence of himself.

THE IMPLICATION OF ALTRUISM.

The great law of Jesus, which in this day is called "altruism," namely, "Thou shalt love thy neighbor as thyself," impliedly makes the love of one's self precede the love of one's neighbor, and to be at once the foundation thereof and the model thereof. A man who neglects himself to improve the spiritual condition of his neighbor, makes a grave mistake. A man who neglects his own family out of philanthropy to his neighbors, is doing wrong. A man who neglects his church for some extra missionary work and plans of his own, is doing wrong. He is reversing the common-sense principle of Christian morals. The best thing a man can do for the world is to cultivate himself in such manner that if all the world followed his example the world would be vastly better.

In the very doing of this a man acquires greater power to help his fellow-men to be better. In caring for his own household he is making a model after which if all the families of the earth lived the whole world would be better; and he is training his family to be more useful to the community to which they belong. His doing good to that which is farthest off does not excuse a man for neglecting that which is nearest him. It was no excuse for John Howard for neglecting his boy at home and letting him grow up to be a moral pest, that the father was looking after the prisoners incarcerated in distant jails of the kingdom. The rule is, *Do* NOW *that which is nearest:* discharge plain duties first, consider probable duties afterward. The doing of the former will give more wisdom and strength for the doing of the latter.

KNOWLEDGE AGGRAVATES SIN.

There is a collateral truth to that which is clearly expressed in the words of our author, and that truth is, *Knowledge aggravates sinfulness.* We cannot dissolve our responsibility by shutting our eyes to our opportunities; on the contrary, if we have any unemployed powers, and there are not opportunities which press themselves upon our attention, we are bound to seek them. Let it never be forgotten what the lord said to his servant who had not improved the one talent: "You ought to have *put out* my money." There is such a thing as economy of a whole life, and that word "economy" is a very comprehensive one. It means a study of the outlay of everything at our command. We are bound to study that there be no waste of physical, intellectual, or spiritual powers. We are to plan that each one shall be employed where and when and how it can do the most good.

No one fails to see the truth of this in finance. A man studies to make an outlay of his money for two purposes, of increasing it and enjoying it. So also should a man study to make an outlay of everything else which may be accounted as among his personal assets. And in the light of that truth follows another, namely, that the sin is always greater when the opportunity is presented to us, and shown to lie within the circle of our ability.

THE MONEY ILLUSTRATION.

There is no illustration so comprehensible to every class of intellect as an illustration taken from money. To apply our principle, let us suppose a person with a very large income. Every cent of any income, great or small, is to be spent for God, because it is God's. The single question in spending any dime or shilling is, Will this have a tendency to make the relationship between God and man a happier and a more improving one? A right-minded man can form the habit of bringing that principle to bear in the decision of every penny he spends for an apple and every dime he spends for a ride, and the principle may obtain such rule over his life that instinctively the question is settled, whether he ought to ride or walk, to eat or abstain. When a man's income is very large this becomes a serious matter, and often makes life burdensome. He cannot content his conscience, unless it be an evil conscience, with assigning to the promotion of influential efforts to do good, so small a proportion of his income as he did when that income was smaller.

For instance, a Christian woman was a milliner in her early married life, and had no income but that which could be allowed her by her Christian husband, who was a mechanic working on wages; the two at the end of the year had very little left after their modest and proper expenses were met, but nevertheless, they contrived to give one-tenth of their income to works of charity beyond their own family. That woman, in after life, was left a widow, with an income of five thousand dollars a month. If she contented herself with giving only five hundred dollars a month to charities, she might be described simply as a poor kind of Christian. Her conscience ought to have told her that she was living daily in sin.

But even if she felt the full force of that, and then endeavored to live simply and quietly and expend her entire income over and above her proper needs on worthy works outside her family, she would soon come to the end of her responsibility. There would be presented to her so many causes that were really worthy, that four thousand dollars a month—four-fifths of her income set aside for charity—would not meet the demands of all. She must then determine for herself *which* of those calls are most binding on her. It is part of her education to determine such questions, and the settlement must be made not on any grounds of selfishness or vanity or other forms of worldliness, but on the simple ground of doing good.

It is not every gift of money that does good. The mode, the direction, and the spirit of the gift have much to do with the result. The very moment it becomes known that a rich man has made a large gift of money there begins the in-pouring of applications from all quarters of the world. It is so even where a man is suspected of being where he can influence the rich. All pastors of men who are known to be wealthy and liberal are deluged with such applications.

A friend of mine, who at the time could have drawn his check for twenty millions of dollars, once offered me five millions of dollars to meet the appeals made upon me for money, if I would give him a guarantee that that, divided up amongst those whom I knew to be needy, and those who knew me, would end all applications. He was a shrewd man; he knew that I knew that if I had all the money in all the banks and vaults in America, it would not achieve that result; that when it came to be known that I had money to distribute, it would set the world howling after me. There must be at least forty millions of people in America who want a little more money for something else. Now, in such a case as this, each person must regulate his outlay wisely, and never give anything, and never do anything, simply to get rid of the solicitors.

FOUR WAYS OPEN TO ALL.

Are you willing and ready to do good as you have opportunity? Have you been interested in what has been written above in regard to persons of large means? And do you say, "I have very little money to give; and I have very little bodily strength; and I have very little intellectual force; and I have a very small circle of influence"? If these things be so, nevertheless, there must be some way in which you can do good, and you must know that way, and if you do not walk therein, remember that you are therefore a sinner. Money is not everything. It has been selected merely as an example. Everything whereby life can be modified comes under the rule. The poorest and feeblest reader of this page can do four things which will be of very great use to the whole world.

(1) *Stand out of the way of workers.* If you cannot do much good, or fancy you can do none, at least do not stand in the way of those who can. In your own family, study how to cease to be an obstruction to those who have some ability to bring people into a better state. Do so in your church. Do so in any society to which you may belong. Everywhere there are people, professing to be Christians, who stand in the way of the world's progress. Every pastor is worried and overworked in striving to climb over or pull aside the dead logs, the almost worthless obstructionists in the church; people who are constantly giving him trouble by their neglect of duties, by their bad tongues, or by the deadening influence of their lethargic lives. If

you cannot help to extinguish a conflagration, for goodness' sake move out of the way of the engines that are flying to the rescue.

(2) *Then lend the whole pressure of your steady influence to the side of right.* It may be a very little pressure. It may be only an ounce, but sixteen such pressures make a pound, and a couple of thousands of such pounds make a ton. You are not responsible for any portion of the pound beyond your sixteenth; but for *that* sixteenth you are responsible. The difference between an influential effort and the steady pressure of influence is very readily perceived. There are useful men who almost never make any effort the effect of which is perceived. They write no book, they deliver no discourse, they contribute no fund that the world, or any portion thereof, perceives and feels instantaneously; but they always stand in with the good; they always stand up for the right; they are always counted for the truth. It was a woman, Hannah More, who invented the phrase, " The logic of the life." It embodies a splendid truth. There are thousands of lives no incident in one of which can be used to illustrate any particular truth, or assist in any particular cause, the sum total of each one of which is an unanswerable argument for the right. If no special passage in your life be so conspicuous as to arrest any man's attention, let your character, as a whole, make an impression for the truth. Let its weight, however

little, press every one it touches away from the wrong and into the right.

(3) *Become a propagandist.* You have some convictions, and there is at least one person with whom you talk sometimes. Endeavor to lay the weight of your convictions of any truth on the soul of your neighbor. Never mention your doubts, unless it be to those who can dissipate them, but always calmly and resolutely stand by your convictions. It will tell in the long run.

(4) *Be good.* There is no way of doing good so thoroughly efficacious as being good. One good man given to a town is better than the gift of a park, or, it may be, of a library. One good man is worth more to a town than a hundred of the most learned men who are not good. One good man does not illuminate every spot along the shore, but he stands as a lighthouse from whose lamp, a foot or two in diameter, a light streams miles far over the dark seas of night, and enables the mariner to guide his bark away from the wrecking rocks.

In all our efforts to be useful let us remember that it is the motive which sanctifies the good deed; that works without faith are dead, even as faith without works is dead. In the Gospel sense, doing good means doing that for others which will enable them to do more to bring their human brothers into happier relations with the Heavenly Father, and so please the Heavenly Father.

XI.

Impending Judgment.

CHAPTER V., 1-6.

A RECALL.

IN coming to study the last chapter in this epistle, we must remind ourselves of the primary design of the writer, namely, to reach those Jews who had become Christians with words of rebuke for the sins of which they had become guilty, and to recall them to the consolations of the Gospel of the blessed God. It does not seem to be an unreasonable or unnatural conjecture that JAMES would suppose that this letter, passing in the autograph or in copies among his scattered parishioners, would also find its way into the hands of Jews who were outside the Christian parish. This would in a measure account for the tone of the opening of the fifth chapter. But it is not necessary to rely upon this alone in accounting for the startling phraseology. It is quite possible that there were rich people as well as poor among Hebrew-Christians. It is not unlikely that some of them had accumulated property by the industrial exercise of their skill in trade. His appeal would be applicable to them. There is also the rhetorical ground: by pointing out the follies and sins of the rich, a preacher or writer gives comfort to those who are poor, and who desire to maintain their integrity by keeping their virtue unbroken.

For so thoughtful a writer as JAMES all these three considerations might have had weight when he wrote the following searching words:

"*Come now, ye rich, ye shouting ones; weep for the miseries coming upon you. Your wealth hath rotted and your garments have become moth-eaten. Your gold and silver are rusted, and their rust shall be for witness unto you, and shall eat your flesh as fire. You have accumulated in the last days. See, the hire of the laborers who have mowed your field, which is kept back by you, crieth out; and the cries of those who have reaped have entered into the ears of the Lord of hosts. You have lived luxuriously upon the earth, and have been sportive and fattened your hearts in a day of slaughter. You have condemned, you have murdered the Just One; He doth not resist you.*"

It would be a great mistake ethically, and be doing great injustice to our author, if any one supposed that he indulged in anything like class-hate, or had any intent to nourish that low and wicked sentiment. There is no virtue nor vice in riches, and equally, no virtue nor vice in poverty. A rich man may be a good man and so may a poor man. The latter may be a bad man and so may a rich man. The rags of Lazarus did not bear him heavenward, neither did the purple and fine linen of Dives draw him hellward. A man's material property is altogether an outward condition. His moral character is altogether an inward estate, and yet, as we can perceive, the character modifies the condition, and the condition may modify the character, for our growth in godliness. As great helps may be found in poverty as in riches. But both may become agencies for our spiritual deterioration. It is wise in any man to be very careful lest his outward condition damage his inward character. It is not having riches, however great, that is hurtful. All the world ought to know that wealth does not make superiority. poverty inferiority; just as wealth cannot procure unalloyed bliss nor poverty make unmitigated evil.

The three most important things about a man's wealth are these: first, How it was obtained; secondly, How it is enjoyed; thirdly, How it is used. Lucre is not filthy itself; but if obtained by unjust means, it becomes filthy lucre; or if it be enjoyed selfishly, lavishly, and carnally, it becomes filthy lucre; or if employed to carry out crafty and wicked designs by corrupting men to become instruments for evil in the hands of its owner, it is filthy lucre.

It is to men who have so obtained and employed wealth that JAMES calls in tones of tremendous warning. In the midst of the shouts of their revelry he calls them to weep, in words spoken in tones of the old prophets. So Isaiah (ch. 13) called to their ancestors, "Hear ye, for the day of the Lord is at hand; it shall come as a destruction from the Almighty, therefore shall all hands be faint and every man's heart shall melt. They shall be amazed, every man at his neighbor; their faces shall be as flames." It is a call to arouse them from their self-contentment and self-sufficiency; dispositions frequently caused by great riches. He prophesies that miseries are coming upon them. He seems to hear the footfall of the approaching days of misery—misery that could not be warded off by all the wealth which they had gathered around them. Scarcely a decade passed before this prophecy was fulfilled. The turbulent disposition of the Jews, their incessant seditions and frequent outbreaks, at last brought upon them the destruction of their city, when, as Josephus informs us, the Zealots spared none but those who were poor and low in fortune, and were so insatiably rapacious that they searched all the houses of the rich, killing the men and abusing the women. And the same writer informs us that these terrors befell not only those who were in Judea, but also those who were "in dispersion." When any day of judgment falls upon a people such as then fell upon the Jews, the whole nation is involved. What then can riches do?

In the picturesque phrases which follow, JAMES alludes to the various kinds of wealth in his day. We must remember that this epistle was written long before corporate combinations, such as now prevail, had entered into the contrivances of men either for the accumulation or for the preservation of their wealth, such as shares of stock in mining companies and railway companies, and what are called "trusts," monopolies, and other modes of investment. Even our modern investment in works of fine art was a thing unknown. If a man acquired wealth beyond his own house and garden, what was he to do with it? There were three classes of things in which he ordinarily invested it, namely, grain, clothes, and gold or silver coin.

The first might be used in several ways. It might be stored for a rise in breadstuffs, something like our modern "corners in grain"; or it might be transported and sold; or it might be kept stored in vaults for the owner's use if there should come at any time a famine or a war. With such wealth one might say, like the man in the parable (Luke 12), who had stored all his goods in the shape of grain: "Soul, thou hast much goods laid up for many years; take thine ease; eat, drink, and be merry." When the calamities came, the grain, which had been kept up at a high price, thus increasing the suffering of the poor, had become rotten in the bins.

Another form of accumulation was in the shape of costly raiment, and even of plainer garments in greater quantities. In our day this kind of accumulation is almost unknown, because the fashions are so constantly varying. But in olden times and even in our own day, the fashions do not change in the East. As the prizes taken in ancient wars, we frequently hear of fine garments as amongst the treasures. It is said that when Alexander the Great took Persepolis the riches of all Asia were gathered there; not only quantities of silver and gold, but also abundance of raiment. When the Roman Lucullus was requested to lend a hundred garments to the theatre, he replied that he had five thousand in his house, and they were welcome to take as many as they would. In regard to that species of wealth, JAMES said, "Your garments have become moth-eaten;" and so he said of coin, "Your gold and silver are rusted." This must, of course, refer to the soil which will gather even upon the precious metals when laid aside, although they could not rust in our modern sense of becoming oxidized. But long kept out of circulation, and thus increasing the embarrassment of society, they had become spotted in the secret and safe places where they had been concealed.

The words of JAMES must have brought back to his Christian readers the exhortation of his great brother: "Lay not up for yourselves treasures upon earth, where moth and rust doth corrupt, and where thieves break through and steal ; but lay up for yourselves treasures in heaven, where neither moth nor rust doth corrupt, and where thieves do not break through nor steal" (Matt. 6) He announced to them that the rust of their money should rise up against them and condemn them, and come down upon them and punish them ; that is, should eat into them, with an agony that should be like the burning of one's flesh ; for their avarice, which had led them to such great injustice, which had warmed their hearts and burned out their neighbors, should be in them like the flaming fire. Here, again, we have the old prophetic thunder, as when the Psalmist said : " Thou shalt make them as a fiery oven in the time of Thy wrath, and the fire shall eat them up" (Ps. 21 : 9). As when Isaiah said, " The Light of Israel shall be for a fire and the Holy One for a flame. It shall burn and eat up; it shall eat up from the soul to the flesh" (Isa. 10 : 16). As when Jeremiah said, " Behold, I will make My word in thy mouth, fire, and the people wood, and it shall eat them up" (Jer. 5 : 14) As when Ezekiel said, " They shall go out from one fire and another fire shall devour them" (Ezek. 15 : 7). " I will bring forth a fire from the midst of thee, and the fire shall eat thee up " (Ezek. 28 : 18).

JAMES was writing to people who were much more familiar with this phraseology than we are in our day. To the Jews who lived when JAMES wrote, this soon came to be literally true; for their substance and their flesh were destroyed when the city and the temple were burned. Josephus tells us that the flames consumed their dead bodies and their substance and their wardrobes. Whatever was spared from the flames fell into the hands of the Romans; and so, it came to pass that the treasures which had been heaped up to prnduce for them a long season of quiet and comfort were all swept away; for they had planted their seed in a garden that lay over the heart of a volcano which was soon to burst. Their doom was aggravated by the injustice which they had used in the accumulation of their hoarded property. They had violated the law of justice and, as well, the law of benevolence, and had broken the precept of Moses in which it was recorded, "The wages of him that is hired shall not abide with thee all night until the morning" (Lev. 19:13). As also, "Thou shalt not oppress a hired servant that is poor and needy at his day, thou shalt give him his hire; neither shall the sun go down upon it, lest he cry against thee to the Lord, and it be a sin unto thee" (Lev. 24:14, 15). This hire, which was still in their possession, the interest of which they had enjoyed, now cried out against them from the secret places where they had stored grain, or garments, or gold, as the blood of Abel cried unto God from the ground against his brother Cain (Gen. 4:10).

Perhaps there is no portion of this denunciation which could be brought home to the modern Christian community more decisively than this. The crying sin against the rich in every large city is the sin of keeping back the hire which belongs to the laborers ; and this is probably committed oftener by Christian women than by Christian men. Amongst us the sin consists in postponing, as a small matter, a small debt to the poor man: a messenger, a porter, a laundress, or some menial. Amongst our ladies, the little bill of the dressmaker or the milliner is little only to the debtor, not to the creditor. The poor working woman has an old mother, or a helpless brother, or a young child to support. Her rent is to be paid exactly at the hour. No grace of time is granted to her, as it is to a man whose rent is twenty thousand dollars a year. She must pay her rent, or have her baby's cradle and her other little furniture put out on the sidewalk. On Saturday night she must pay for the meat and the flour which have been bought during the week, or she and her loved ones must fast through the Sunday, and fast on until her rich sister, who wears the work produced by weary fingers and sometimes wet with bitter tears, shall think of her little bill, and pay it. Oh, my sisters, this is a crying sin of this day. In this great city in which I am writing, last Sunday, hundreds of ladies swept magnificently dressed into the House of God, and quietly sat in their pews under the preaching, and went out to sumptuous dinners, and rested delicately for their afternoon's *siesta* on soft couches, while their poor laboring sisters were compelled to stay from church because some little bill was not paid; and that little bill was not paid on Saturday because, when the poor work-woman called, the debtor was chatting pleasantly with some flattering friend, and sent word to the poor woman to come again; or else, had gone riding into the park, and forgot to leave the amount which she had promised should be paid on Saturday. If any Christian man or woman shall read this passage on Sunday when he owes fifty cents, or a dollar, or two, or three, or five dollars, anything under ten dollars, to any man or woman known to be poor, let him close this volume at this page and go out, Sunday as it is, and hunt up his little creditor, and pay that little bill, lest the angel of death come upon him this day, and he go to the judgment-seat with this corroding sin eating in upon his moral nature. Let him make no hypocritical defence that it is Sunday. Sunday? Why better than any prayer that you can offer in the closet, at the family-altar, or in the church, would be this deed of simple justice. Your debt of twenty-five thousand dollars down on the exchange can stand over until to-morrow, but the hire of the laborer which you have kept back *cries!* And the cry hath entered into the ears of the Lord of hosts.

Let that tremendous name shake your conscience to its very centre. You may be too superb to pay attention to the small debt due your neighbor; but God is so great that He can pay attention to the least of things. We may be so self-absorbed as to be able to listen only to some great news, some great scheme, some great thought ; but God is so great that into His ear enters the sigh, not to say the cry, of the poor field hand, the poor needle-worker, sent up from barn or from garret unto Him. And little and needy as the sufferer is, the Lord who hears him, let us remember, is the "Lord of hosts," the Lord that commands all the physical forces and all the spiritual dynamics of the universe, the Lord who can bring to the rescue of the lowliest every power that makes and shapes and shakes the universe which He hath created.

In addition to covetousness and oppression, JAMES presents to their conscience the sin of voluptuousness. There is nothing in any part of Holy Scripture to teach that there is any wrong in the rational enjoyment of the legitimate pleasures of this pleasant life. On the contrary, the Scriptures confirm the teachings of nature, namely, that the Heavenly Father is provident of His children, making all nature serve them ; not bringing them upon the planet until all arrangements had been made, so that a race of human beings, living properly, would exist in a condition of perfect physical, intellectual, and spiritual comfort. His storing of the coal in the cellar of the mansion of man, that it might afford heat for his body, fire for his kitchen, illumination for his nights, and steam for his progress, is ample proof of this. The obvious intent of the Creator, as all His plans do show, is that His children may be happy. His moral law shows the same thing. Nothing is put about a child of God to fence him in; but everything to fence destruction out. The moral law is not a prison but a fortress.

And so the Gospel of the Blessed God shows us that, even when we had gone out and exposed ourselves to the extremest spiritual calamity, God so loved the world that He gave His only-begotten Son, that whosoever believeth in Him should not perish, but have everlasting life. He desires that we shall see life, that we shall have life and have it more abundantly. His disposition toward us is declared in the statement of the Apostle, that "He giveth us all things richly to enjoy." Supposing a certain amount of enjoyment to be possible to any one man in his lifetime, it is plain that the excesses of one day make drafts upon another day; it may be, upon all days. If he have a thousand days to live and ten thousand dollars be put at his command, it is plain that he will have the purchasing power of ten dollars for every day in his life. But if he spend fifty dollars a day in the first hundred days, it is quite plain that he would have less than six dollars a day during the remaining nine hundred. And if he spend a hundred dollars a day for the first hundred days, the remaining nine hundred would be spent in absolute penury. This is a rigid mathematical calculation, which does not do justice to the case, for life is composed of so many factors, and each man has so many faculties and connections that an impairment of a man is a wider injury than the removal of anything which can be represented by numbers.

To these destructive excesses great wealth tempts any man, no matter what may be his moral qualities. The persons whom JAMES addressed had been living in this extravagant, voluptuous way, which made earth their home, a home they desired to live in forever; which made work and duty disagreeable to them; which had brought them to a state of mind that engaged all their faculties in discovering modes of enjoyment, rather than methods of usefulness. And so, their lives had come to be beastly, as beasts are fed in the stalls and fattened for the day when they are to be slaughtered; and so, the highest characteristic of their whole nature was this, that they were simply *fit to be killed*. We find, in our own day, that men of enormous wealth do often spend their money in such a fashion that, while it fattens their hearts, it brings on the day of their doom.

The luxury of the rich Jews, in the time of JAMES,

was like that of their forefathers, as described by the prophet Amos (6:4), "*That lie upon beds of ivory, and stretch themselves upon their couches, and eat the lamb out of the flock, and the calves out of the midst of the stall; that chant to the sound of the viol, and invent to themselves instruments of music like David; that drink wine in bowls, and anoint themselv s with chief ointments; but they are not grieved for the affliction of Joseph!*"

The result in the days of Amos, as that in the days of JAMES, will always be the result of such a course of conduct. Whenever Church people indulge the pleasures of the flesh to such a degree that they become careless as to the condition of the Church, whenever it does not make them mourn that religion is languishing and sin is prevailing, then their pleasures become their snare, and their bodily enjoyment will end in the spiritual death.

The fourth sin with which JAMES charges the rich, the worldly, and the wanton Jews of his day, is the oppression of the righteous, even to the taking of their lives. The phrase, "the just," which he uses in verse 6, has received many interpretations. One takes it to mean that whole body of people who had fallen under the hatred of the Jews, from whom they had separated themselves; the latter had the power of money to follow up, to harass, and to destroy those whom they hated for ecclesiastical reasons. Their general disposition was hatred to the good; their general course of conduct, the destruction of the good. But there can be no objection, it would seem, to translating it "the Just One," and applying the phrase to our Lord Jesus Christ, JAMES knew that Stephen had charged the Council with murdering "the Just One" (Acts 7: 62), that "the Just One" was the title given to our Lord (Acts 3: 14, and 22: 14), and that their crime in murdering Jesus was presented as all the more atrocious because He had rightfully claimed to be their Messiah. He seems to be echoing again the words of Jesus, who told the Jews of His generation, that upon them was to come all the righteous blood shed from the days of Abel to the days of Zacharias.

If the application of the verse be made either to the good in general, or to the Lord Jesus Christ in particular, there is something very striking in the omission of the conjunction. "Ye have condemned, ye have killed, the Just," expresses the rapidity of the action and result of their maliciousness. They seemed to be so afraid that after condemning a good man He should escape slaughter, that they hurried up His death, although, as a lamb before the shearers is dumb, He opened not His mouth. There is a touch of sweetness in the title which JAMES gives to his crucified Brother—"The Just One," for he himself, among his people, had gone by the name of "JAMES the Just." But his slain Brother had become his risen Lord, and by His resurrection and ascension had so established the justice of His claims to the Messiahship, that ever hereafter JAMES would transfer the title to Jesus, and have Jesus known as "the Just One," amongst all the just upon the face of the earth, in all the ages of the history of mankind.

XII.

The Final Theme.

CHAPTER V., 7-20.

THE FINAL THEME: PATIENCE.

JAMES now approaches the final theme of his epistle in an address to his Christian brethren. The connection seems to be that, since such great miseries are to come upon their persecutors, they may well be exhorted to endurance and patience. He turns from his address to the un-Christian Jews to speak to his own brethren, to those who were bound to him not only by the tie of nationality but by their being members of the family of the Lord Jesus Christ.

"*Be patient, therefore, brethren, until the coming of the Lord. Behold, the tiller of the ground waiteth for the valued fruit of the ground, being patient over it, until he receives the rain, the early and the latter. Be ye also patient; strengthen your hearts; for the coming of the Lord is at hand. Do not complain one against another, brethren, that ye be not condemned. Behold, the Judge standeth before the doors.*"

The word which we translate "patient" has a many-sided meaning. It means a readiness to suffer long. It means the resistance of our natural impatience for a long season. It means a persistent endurance of painful experience. It means courage, forbearance, magnanimity, the knowing how "to suffer and be strong." It does not mean unfeelingness, nor stoicism. It means quiet endurance for a sufficient reason.

THE COMING OF THE LORD.

The reason assigned is *that the Lord is coming*. He is coming to be present upon earth. This was a doctrine held in all apostolic times, and shines through all the New Testament Scripture, as in prophecy it shone through all the Old Testament. As the predictions of the Old Testament were fulfilled when the Lord Jesus Christ made His appearance in the flesh at the incarnation, so will all predictions of the New Testament be fulfilled when the Lord shall come again.

The certain thing is that He will come. The uncertain thing is *when* He will come, and these two combine to keep our faith and patience up to their highest point. If the Lord delay His coming year after year and century after century our faith would utterly fail us, unless we had the certainty that He *would* come. Again, if we undertake to fix the date by any sort of application of mathematics to prophecy, and there be any fault in our figuring, there will also come a failure of our faith. All we can do is to stand by the assertion of the Sacred Scriptures, "He is coming," looking forward in the sure faith and cheering hope that *there is to be another epiphany of Jesus.*

Our author may have applied the phrase to the coming of the Lord to destroy the city of Jerusalem and sweep away the old Mosaic institutions; as we now know that "coming of the Lord" did bring upon the wicked, rich Jews those miseries which JAMES told them were coming upon them. But to the faithful, in all ages, there have been events which may be very properly called, "comings of the Lord." Surely, when a Christian man closes his career at death there is a coming of the Lord. He hath promised that He will come again and take us unto Himself, that where He is, there we may be also (John 14).

THE EXAMPLE OF THE FARMER.

Then JAMES encourages his brethren to patience by the example of the husbandman. The tiller of the soil plows his field, casts therein his precious seed-corn, and leaves it there, and waits till it shall come to fruition. Waits for the rain, for the early rain and the latter rain He waited for the Autumn rain before he sowed; he waits for the Spring rain before he gathers. He knows the preciousness of the fruit that shall come. He depends upon it for his livelihood, and for seed for the next year's sowing. He knows that he cannot hasten the ripening of his crop by affecting in any degree the sunshine or the rain; but he also knows that, according to the laws of nature, seed placed in the earth and rained upon and sunned, will come to growing crops. So surely does a faithful man know that the good seed which he is sowing in faith may lie in the ground for many, many days; but the law in the spiritual world just as firmly holds as in the natural; and the harvest will come.

TIME A FACTOR.

Wherefore JAMES exhorts his brethren to strengthen their hearts, considering that their sufferings cannot be long, and the Lord will not stay away one single hour beyond the time when the rescue of His servants demands His presence. One thing quite necessary for a high moral character is to *take the factor of time into account*. It does so much every way. It loosens and tightens, it lifts up and casts down, it straightens and rectifies, or, at least, it seems to do so, because the operations of the active physical and spiritual forces of the universe require time as certainly as they require space. When Christian people are under the influence of thoughts like these, while they are suffering they may abstain from sighing and from groaning, from murmuring, complaining, fault-finding, grudging, all which things are contained in the injunction, "Do not complain one against another, brethren."

THE SIN OF GRUMBLING.

Do Christian people quite sufficiently consider the sin of grumbling, the sin of being discontented with the allotment of Providence, as to the time and place of their birth; as to the family in which they were born; as to their environment, as well as their heredity? What a strange sight a grumbling Christian is! He is a man who believes that God hath forgiven his sins, that Christ hath borne them all away, that his Lord has gone to prepare a place for him, that in a short time he will be where neither pain nor persecution can reach him, where the load of life will be laid down, where the wicked shall cease from troubling and the weary shall be forever at rest. And yet he allows small and transient things to keep him awake in the night, to worry him, and make him peevish and fretful and cross through the day. He makes his own burdens more distressing by fretting under them, and thus increases the burdens which his friends have to bear. How many Christians fail to put their grumblings into the category of their sins. But JAMES'S admonition, that we should not grumble lest we be damned, ought to arouse us to the duty of being patient, and to the fact that all really true Christian faith increases a man's manliness.

He both warns and encourages by the fact that the Judge is standing before the very doors. He hears everything that is said, and He knows, while He stands at the door, that He has a dear friend within, a friend who is suffering, ah, what bodily, what mental pains, and yet, in memory of the sufferings of his Lord, with faith in the knowledge and sympathy of his Lord, is sitting in silence and bearing it all, even as his Lord in *His* agony "opened not His mouth."

THE EXAMPLE OF THE PROPHETS.

He draws another incentive to patience and dissuasive from grumbling from the example of the good men who have lived in other ages.

"*As an example of suffering evil and of patience, my brethren, take the prophets who have spoken in the name of the Lord. Behold, we call them blessed who endured. You have heard of the endurance of Job and have seen the end of the Lord; for very compassionate is the Lord and merciful.*"

Encouragement may be found for those in suffering by reviewing the lives of the greatest and the best men that ever lived. They have never been found amongst those who were wicked and wanton, pleasure-seekers and at ease. The greatest line of men known to those to whom the epistle was addressed were the prophets, whose careers are set forth in the Old Testament Scripture. Were any of them easy-going men? Did their eyes stand out with fatness? Did they have every pleasure the flesh desired? Were their days spent with wine and their nights with women? Were they clothed in purple and fine linen? Did their mountains stand strong and their homes abide? No, every one of them was a man harassed, persecuted, chased. They were strangers and pilgrims in the earth. They forsook the homes of their childhood and the graves

of their fathers, and went into strange countries.
They left the fields that were rich and went to
lands where they must toil. They were tortured,
they had trials of mockings and scourgings; they
had bonds and imprisonments; they were stoned
and torn asunder; they went about in sheep-
skins and goat-skins, wandering in deserts and
mountains, and caves, and the holes of the earth.
They were destitute and afflicted. They were
stoned and sawn asunder, and slain with the
sword. Who are *we*, that we should expect to
obtain the crowns which they wear, if we be unwilling to fight the battles which they fought?
And *now* we call them "blessed." If they had
failed, if they had cast the burden down, if they
had refused the fight, if they had fled from the
cross, no one would consider them "blessed."
They would have failed to gain immortal fame.

AN ILLUSTRIOUS GENTILE SUFFERER.

He recalled to them the example of an illustrious Gentile sufferer. Job was not always patient in the sense of being speechless. Sometimes his agonies were so great and so greatly
increased by the torturing company of his friends,
that they wrung from him cries that have sound-
ed through all history down to our days. And
yet he suffered and suffered, concluding every
wail of his spirit with words which expressed the
deepest sentiment of his soul: "Though He
slay me, yet will I trust in Him." In the days

of JAMES, the Jewish Christians, it is said, gave special honor to the name of Job. Saint as he was, he suffered. Suffering, therefore, is not incompatible with sainthood.

There seems to be one other sentiment in these words, namely, that no suffering can be so long continued that it will not come to an end; that no waves can break over a man so as to drown him utterly out of the sight of God; and that the greater and longer the suffering which any man endures, the more complete and illustrious is the demonstration which the conclusion thereof affords the world when the Lord brings it to an end, and crowns it with the great glory. Such men become monumental, and guide the march of humanity down the centuries.

AGAINST OATHS.

As our author is drawing to the close of his epistle he gives his brethren several directions, the observance of which would lead to an increase of their patience. The first of these is that striking precept in the 12th verse:

"*But before all, brethren mine, do not swear, neither by heaven nor by earth, nor by any other object of oath; but be your yes, yes, and your no, no; that you fall not under condemnation.*"

No reader can fail to hear in these words another echo of the words of Jesus as they are recorded in Matt. 5: 34-37. While this injunction covers the whole ground of profanity, it may be supposed to have been intended for JAMES's earlier readers, to warn them against certain evils into which their trials for the sake of the faith were liable to plunge them, and which may recur from age to age to all who are striving to serve the Lord Jesus in simplicity and godly sincerity.

VOWS IN TROUBLE.

(1) It has not been an uncommon thing for men to take vows in trouble, as if they would do them any good. They have promised if certain ends could be attained to pursue certain courses of life; and sometimes, to give a supposed greater efficacy, they have bound themselves with oaths. The Hebrew-Christians in the first century were peculiarly exposed to this. The evil of it lay in transferring their confidence from the grace and power of God to the vows which they were making, and thus begetting in them a strong tendency to confidence in magic. With us the evil may come up just as with them. At times when men have been caught in exceedingly tight places by reason of their imprudence or their sins, in times when men have fallen into great bodily pain, they have thoughtlessly sworn that if God would deliver them out of the pressing difficulties they would change their whole course of life. The evil of this lies in the supposition, that if they be not delivered as they desire they are not bound to dedicate themselves to God's service. It is on that supposition these men have been living before their difficulties came. If they be extricated, it is so

easy to forget the vow and return to the old modes of life. If a man vow, he should pay his vow unto the Lord. It is, however, better never to make a vow, but to walk the path of duty dutifully. It is as if JAMES has said, " Brethren, do not vow that if this storm could be lifted from your sky you will be more faithful Christians ; you are bound to be faithful as it is, and to trust God's goodness and mercy to shorten or lengthen your sufferings as may be best."

There may be something in this injunction applicable to our modern temperance pledges. A man addicted to strong drink, and feeling the degradation of the slavery into which he has gone, signs a vow that he will never drink intoxicants. How worthless such pledges are is well known both to those who make and those who administer them. The will-power necessary to keep such a pledge is sufficient to enable a man to break the habit without such a pledge. If he have not that power, he will certainly violate his pledge, and thus hurt himself by overloading with falsehood and a sense of failure, a spirit already weakened by sinful indulgences. Better not " swear off," but break off. Instead of swearing that you will never drink again, pray for grace to keep you from ever drinking again, and continue to pray and abstain until the habit be broken.

DISOWNING THE CHRISTIAN PROFESSION.

(2) It may have been a warning to them, not to swear when they were brought before Roman

magistrates, or were in the company of pagan persecutors, in order to show by such words that they were not Christians. The whole world from the beginning, had supposed that no follower of so holy a person as Jesus would indulge in profane language. This was so early and so well known that, when, on the last night of Christ's suffering, Peter was charged with being one of His followers, he broke into profane expressions, and he knew that that would be an argument to convince them that he was not a Christian. And it did.

CONJURATION.

(3) The injunction might have applied to the temptation there was among them to conspire together in sworn bands against their persecutors; as was frequently the case in their own age and has been ever since. In our English tongue "conjuration" once meant banding together with oaths and not, as now, attempts at magical processes. JAMES saw the futility of all seditious movements. He saw that it plunged his brethren only into deeper and deeper troubles; wherefore, he besought them not to seek such modes of relief, not to bind themselves to others, or others to themselves, in order to effect deliverance, but to put all in the hand of God.

PROFANITY.

(4) But whether any or all of these considerations were in the mind of our author, it is quite

certain that he pronounced a very emphatic denunciation against profanity. His opening phrase shows the depth of his convictions. Why, before all things, must they guard against profanity, if profanity itself be not an exceedingly heinous offence? It is such, lightly as it is esteemed, even in what is called "good society." In Christian countries at this day, it is a dire and dreadful vice. Men take the name of the Most High in vain, using it lightly, perhaps, at first, under the conviction that it gives strength to their rhetoric, and thus glide into a vice which saps the moral constitution. The sin of common profanity, or swearing, is a sin against God and against one's self. It is a sin against God, because it deprives Him of the honor due His name, and is in direct disobedience to His commandment, which sets forth His opinion of such language in the most explicit form: "Thou shalt not take the name of the Lord thy God in vain, for the Lord will not hold him guiltless that taketh His name in vain."

The sin is not mitigated by modifications of phraseology. Even in what is called good society in England it is not uncommon to hear the phrase, "by Jove," a phrase sometimes employed by young Americans who are fond of aping Anglican manners, interlarding the speech of men, young and old, introduced carelessly without regard to rhetoric or to sense. One may as well swear " by God's wounds " as " by Zounds," and " Gosh," and " Golly," and " Jeminy " are rustic synonymes for the names of our Creator and Saviour.

ITS HURTFULNESS.

We need not push our reasoning any further in this direction ; it is enough that God condemns it. If I know what is offensive to my dearest friend, I avoid it ; if I know what is disgusting to my most powerful friend, I guard my habits of speech in his presence ; if I am accustomed to the forbidden words, it is enough for me to know that God hates the profanation of His name, to make me avoid using it carelessly on frivolous occasions. In the next place, it is hurtful to any man to become an habitual swearer. It is an effectual bar to his ever being great. It is utterly impossible, whatever other gifts and opportunities be afforded, that a man shall ever reach the utmost possible greatness of humanity, who himself fails to have reverence for that which is great. Reverence is the spring of all aspiration ; reverence is the foundation for all lofty upbuilding of character.

Not only is irreverence to be avoided, but reverence is to be cultivated, that reverence which has a profound respect for all that is lofty in thought, in emotion, in existence. Now, it is manifestly impossible for any man to cultivate reverence for anything, who has no reverence for the highest thing. The thought of God, as Daniel Webster said, is the greatest thought which has entered into the mind of man. When in his common conversation, on trivial occasions, a man plucks down that loftiest thought and spits upon it, he deprives himself of any possibility of rising to lofty intellectual and moral heights. This should be pressed upon the attention of every man, especially upon the young, that they may not fall into this degrading habit.

ITS UTTER USELESSNESS.

The injunction of JAMES is enforced when we consider the *utter uselessness* of a vice which is disgusting to God and degrading to man. It is a gratuitous sin. Murder, adultery, and robbery may be committed under the stimulus of a passionate excitement; but when a man uses profane language, he goes out of his way to pay an unsolicited compliment to the devil. Stealing may enrich a man, murder may gratify his thirst of vengeance, but profanity brings him nothing. No one respects him more for swearing. Although a solemn judicial oath increases confidence in the word of a man, who proceeds to give testimony thereafter, profane swearing diminishes respect for his truthfulness. A man who will thus swear will lie. If he do not observe the most solemn of God's commandments, he is not liable to observe any other. If he takes the name of the Lord in vain, what is to prevent his bearing false witness? If he do not regard what is due to God, will he respect what is due to man?

When, in conversation, a man states something as a fact, and then says, "I swear it is so," even when he does not use the name of God, the hearer naturally has his faith in the statement weakened. If a speaker has no confidence in his own plain statement, how should he expect others to have? The added phrase, "I swear it is so," is indicative of the wavering of his faith in himself. When a man is so notoriously careful of his speech that his affirmation may be always understood to be affirmation and his denial to be denial, those who are acquainted with him have a constantly increasing confidence in his assertions.

Surely of all people Christians should be the most reverent, because God has revealed Himself to them, not only in all the most solemn aspects of His character, as He has to other peoples, but also in all the most tender characteristics of His nature. The God who is in Christ reconciling the world unto Himself ought to be a God before whom all the world should stand in worshipful homage. There is a remarkable passage in Hosea (4:2): "By swearing, and lying, and killing, and stealing, and committing adultery, they break out, and blood toucheth blood," or, as it might be translated, "bloods touch bloods." This shows how the whole line of crimes follows when reverence for God is removed.

JUDICIAL OATHS.

The principle which lies at the root of this, plainly points to the importance of guarding against the multiplication of even judicial oaths. Men brought to give testimony upon frivolous questions should not be put to the test of the oath. Our courts of law would soon begin to find that if testimony were taken upon a simple affirmation of the witness there would be as good an opportunity of reaching the truth as now; and that when the temptation to prevaricate or lie under oath came to a man, it could be more easily resisted if he had not been accustomed to swear over and over again in matters of small importance.

PRAYER CURE.

After warning his brethren against profanity and teaching them to cultivate a hallowed spirit in general, JAMES turns to some directions to them when they are personally in trouble or physically sick.

"*Is any one among you suffering evil? Let him pray. Is any cheerful? Let him sing. Is any sick? Let him call for the Elders of the congregation; and let them pray over him, having anointed him with oil in the name of the Lord; and the prayer of faith shall help the sick and th' Lord shall raise him up; and although he have committed sins it shall be forgiven him.*"

To Christians, as to other men, there come varieties of moods and conditions. Sometimes they are afflicted, sometimes they are prospering, and so, sometimes they are sad, and sometimes they are glad. What shall a Christian do when he is suffering evil or enduring any kind of affliction? Let him not grumble nor be peevish; let him not break forth into profanity; let him pray. Communion with God, fellowship with the Heavenly Father; this is the best comfort in trouble. On the other hand, are his affairs such as make him cheerful? Let him not go into a riot, nor the companionship of wassailers. Let him break forth into song, and let those songs not be gay and giddy ditties, but psalms of praise and thanksgiving and grateful love. Christian people should have their memories stored with the very best parts of the Psalms of David, and other hymns of prayer and praise, as the Apostle Paul wrote to the Colossians (3 : 16), "Let the word of Christ dwell in you richly; in all wisdom teaching and admonishing yourselves, with psalms and hymns and spiritual songs singing; with grace in your hearts unto God." There is no restriction here to any particular psalms, although those of David were generally known to the persons to whom JAMES wrote, and were in Hebrew distinguished as Shurim, Tehillim, and Mizmorim. There were undoubtedly other psalms and hymns and spiritual songs known to him, which have not come down to our day. The teaching of the Apostle is, that instead of any profane, worldly, and frivolous comforts in affliction and in joy, Christians should find sacred modes of expressing their sentiments and comforting their hearts.

THE EARLY CHURCH ORDER.

We now come to a direction of the Apostle which points back to certain things in the origin of the Christian Church, which demand careful consideration. The ideas ordinarily attached to the word "Church" in modern times do not seem to have entered into the minds of the Apostles or of the early Christians. It grew up from small beginnings, in the early centuries, until it consolidated itself into the hard forms in which it stands in modern times. There seems to have been no such thing as an incorporated body to which whosoever belonged was a saved man, and failure of membership in which involved spiritual destruction. Those who loved Jesus for His personality, who received Him as the Messiah of God, adored Him as the spiritual ruler of the universe, and trusted Him as the Savior of their souls, naturally came together. There was one doctrine, namely, the resurrection of Jesus from the dead. They did not speak of "doctrines," as if there were more than one. Those who believed that Christ had raised Himself by the power of God from the dead, therewith drew into their creed every other thing which was necessary to be believed for the regeneration of their lives and the guidance of their moral conduct.

As soon as there was any considerable number of such people, there would naturally be persons who would discharge representative duties, persons to whom some power would be delegated by the congregation for executive purposes. They were the Presbyters. Of these there would naturally be a president, one who should have the oversight of the whole congregation. An overseer, "episcopos" in the Greek tongue, was one who episcopated, that is, *kept oversight*, and hence, the president of the Presbyters was the Bishop of the congregation. A Bishop does not seem to have extended his oversight beyond his own congregation, so that in New Testament language a Bishop is what we call a Pastor. The Presbyters might rotate in the office, or they might all of them fall back into the general congregation, and other brethren take their places, the only office for life being that of the Apostle, which expired when the last man who had seen the risen Jesus and been by Him called to the Apostleship, departed from this world. This is the short and simple statement of what we know of the early Christian Society.

CHARISMATA.

In the early "Church" there were certain spiritual gifts, sometimes called *charismata;* a word which sheds very little light upon the thing itself. After all that has been written on this subject, Neander is most probably nearly right when he gives the definition of the *charisma* as *a capacity in which the power and activity of the indwelling Spirit are revealed.* Whether this capacity had been immediately imparted by the Holy Spirit, or was merely a natural capacity sanctified and enlarged by the principle of the new life, the Holy Spirit so operated upon men, for the edification of Christian people, as to furnish them with a new power to use their natural endowments for the upbuilding of the "congregation."

There is an enumeration of these gifts in First Corinthians 12; in Ephesians 4, and in Romans 12. In the first passage, it is said of Christ, that H "gave some to be Apostles, and some prophets, and some evangelists, and some pastors and teachers." In First Corinthians 12, in addition to those just mentioned, it is said that to each one "is given" the manifestation of the Spirit "to profit withal." Then follows a list including "preaching" and "teaching" and to those are added "to another faith in the same Spirit, and to another the gift of healing in the one Spirit, and to another working of miracles, and to another discerning of spirits, and to another divers kinds of tongues, and to another the interpretation of tongues."

In the close of the chapter, Paul gives another catalogue: "God hath set some in the congregation (Church); first, Apostles; secondly, prophets ; thirdly, teachers ; then miracles ; then gifts of healings, helps, governments, divers kinds of tongues." Perhaps the Presbyters in that early day enjoyed all these extraordinary gifts in their body, some having one and some another ; we do not know whether any one person exhibited all the gifts. And perhaps they were selected from the congregation of believers because they had these spiritual gifts. Whether that be so or not, it is plain that the chief gift was to be an "Apostle," laying the foundation of the faith where it never had been built before. Next in rank and importance was "preaching," the power to set forth the salvation of God in such a way as to persuade men to come into its enjoyment. Next the building up of Christians upon their most holy faith by teaching the things of the Spirit to the children of God. After that, not numbered nor ranked, follow those other things.

DIRECTIONS TO THE SICK.

JAMES comes now to give a direction to those who are sick, and it may be well to impress the very first thing which he says upon the attention of all Christians who fall into sickness, and to present it in the light not simply of a privilege but of a moral duty. The first thing the sick man was to do was to "*send* for the Elders" of the congregation to which he belonged, not of any other congregation. Amongst them would be found some who had the gift of healing. Any one such man would know, upon coming into the presence of the sick man, whether or not he ought to pray for his recovery. This the Apostle calls the gift of "faith." The Holy Spirit would so impress the Elder that he would know that it was God's will that this invalid should be restored; and he might then pray for him. In that case the positive promise was that the man should be restored. In such case the man should be miraculously healed. There is no injunction as to anointing with oil. It is assumed that they would do this, because it was customary in that time that there should be such anointings. They were frequent in the old dispensation, and passed over into the new.

The twelve earliest preachers of the Gospel were accustomed to anoint, as we learn from Mark (6: 13). As a sanitary agent, pure, rich oil, used as an unguent, is healthy, and has been employed by all nations in all times for hygienic purposes. It has been stated in our day, that one of the best cures for scarlet fever is, to take the skin from a freshly boiled ham, with the fat on it, and with it rub the whole person of the invalid. In the case stated by JAMES, it does not appear whether or not the oil was relied upon at all as a remedial agent.

The injunction here is, that after the Elders had anointed the sick man, which any friend in that country would have done, then they should pray with him, and the promise was, that the prayer of faith should help, and heal, and save that sick person; that "the Lord should raise him up." This was a miraculous cure.

SICKNESS AND SIN.

There is one other thing to be noticed in this. The root of all sickness, primarily, is sin. The general sinfulness of our nature crops out in our infirmities. Particular sicknesses also are the fruits of particular sins. It was promised, in case the man had sinned, for whom the Elders were under the direction of God to pray, that the sin should at the same time be pardoned, and that God's healing work would be done thoroughly in soul and body, as when Jesus said to the man who was healed, "Go in peace, and sin no more." This gift of miraculous insight and healing, like all other things necessary for laying the foundations of the faith in the beginning, has now passed away. Indeed these gifts were not continued amongst Christians very long after the time in which JAMES wrote. He himself had been called to the Presbyterate and chosen to the Pastorate, although apparently never assigned to the work of the Apostolate.

But although the particular form set forth by JAMES be not continued among Christians to this day, there is nothing in Holy Scripture or Christian history to forbid the supposition, that from time to time there have occurred certain indications that God so bestowed the "gifts" on certain individuals, under certain circumstances, as to keep alive amongst His people a knowledge of His great power and the desire to cultivate their faith in God.

From time to time there have been occurrences which seemed to show this very plainly. So far as they have come to the personal knowledge of the writer of these pages, or have been so narrated to him as to appear to be entirely credible, these three things seem to have always concurred when the Presbyter has been called: First, the impression has been powerfully made that prayer should be offered for the entire recovery of the patient. Secondly, the patient has concurred in this impression and united in the prayer for his own recovery. Thirdly, the person so recovered was duly and truly penitent of all his sins and seeking forgiveness for them as a thing much more important than his restoration to physical health.

LUTHER'S PRAYER FOR MYCONIUS.

There is nothing in reason, nothing in common sense, nothing in the word of God to set aside the belief, that now, from time to time, God will, in answer to prayer, raise up a man from sickness unto perfect health. It is told that when Myconius lay apparently dying, he wrote a letter to his friend Luther, who, after reading the letter, immediately fell on his knees and began to pray. "O Lord, my God! no, Thou must not take yet our brother, Myconius, to Thyself; Thy cause will not prosper without him. Amen!" And after praying thus, he rose up, and wrote to his sick brother, "There is no cause for fear, dear Myconius; the Lord will not let me hear that thou art dead. You shall not and must not die. Amen!" There words made a powerful impression on the heart of the dying Myconius, and *aroused him in such a manner that the ulcer in his lungs discharged itself*, and he recovered. "I wrote to you that it would be so," answered Luther to the letter which announced the recovery of his friend.

But there is nothing in reason, or common sense, or Holy Scripture, to justify the setting up of faith-shops and the peddling out of faith-cures and the neglect of known remedial agents. There is nothing to justify the belief that, when *any* body anoints *any* body else who is sick and asks for his recovery, that recovery would be guaranteed. If that were so, death would soon be banished from the planet. Even if every time a holy man prayed for another holy man that was sick, for his recovery and the continuance of his beneficent presence amongst his followers, that prayer were obliged to be granted, a physical immortality would have been given to Moses and Elijah, to David and Isaiah, amongst the Israelites, and to the long line of holy workers in the Christian era. If that were so, John Wesley and George Whitfield, Martin Luther and John Calvin, would be alive to-day, and your father and mother, and mine, and multitudes of the godly whom the world has not willingly "let die."

GIVING UP THE GHOST.

We must not leave this thing without calling to our minds the general law of the effect of spirit upon matter. It is very certain that a man may depress his physical constitution by bad habits of the mind, or he may quicken it by the healthful employment of his mental faculties and the wise direction of the actions of his will. Many a man has died when he might have lived if he had positively refused "to give up the ghost." Each man's moral duty is to hold on to "the ghost." No man has a right to die in any sense which involves his own volition. In that single sentence is contained the truth which makes the immorality of suicide. By the force of his will a man must drive all his energies to the defence of the weak spot in his bodily constitution, and repair the waste places by mind-operation. There is that which physiologists have called, "*Vis medicatrix naturæ*," some physical force which of itself heals wounds without external application. There is also a "*Vis medicatrix mentis*," a force of the mind, which goes toward repairing the wastes of the intellect. These two forces may operate antagonistically or in conjunction.

So far as there is a will power in him, each man is bound to help in the invigoration of those two forces.

EXTREME UNCTION.

Whether there be any physical or spiritual help in the anointing of a man who is dying, uniting that anointing with prayer, as in the case of "extreme unction" among our Roman Catholic brethren, we may have to say only this, that this passage of Scripture has nothing whatever to do with it, because in this case the man was anointed and prayed over with the certain expectation that he was to live; whereas, the official of the Roman Catholic Church would, it is presumed, never administer extreme unction except in a case where it was believed that a man was about to die. It is then administered as a preparation for his death; whereas, in the case supposed by our author, it is administered as a preparation for the patient's living.

DUTY OF THE SICK PARISHIONER.

Before parting with this subject entirely, let attention be called to the fact that JAMES directs the sick man to *send* for the official of his own congregation to give him pastoral care. To us in modern times, this lays down a principle which should be duly considered by parishioners and their pastors. *It is the duty of the parishioner when taken sick to send for his pastor.* It is certainly a shame to a Christian man to send for his physician and not send for his pastor. The pastor and the physician must each determine when and how often the visit is to be repeated. It is a very great shame to a parishioner if he complain that his pastor has not visited him in his sickness when he has not sent for that pastor. It is a shame that the invalid depends upon the pastor's missing him from the congregation and hunting him up or upon the pastor's learning of his sickness from some word passing around the church. It is a shame if the sick parishioner send for the pastor of some other congregation. The wrong of this lies in the fact, that it burdens a pastor upon whom he has no claim, and hurts a pastor who has claims upon him. No one should remain in a congregation in whose pastor he has not such confidence, and for whom he has not such love as would lead him to desire to see that pastor so soon as he would desire to see his physician.

It is a question whether a pastor ought to go to see a parishioner whom he incidentally learns to be sick. If that parishioner has not enough confidence in him and love for him to wish to see him in sickness, why should the pastor go? Can he do such a patient any good?

Pastors are engaged in the cure of souls as physicians are engaged in the cure of bodies. When a man is sick he needs both; he wants the mental energy and the physical energy equally stimulated, helped, and guided. Might it not be wholesome if pastors would everywhere announce to their congregations that when they hear of the sickness of their parishioners they may be most careful to keep away until sent for, although where there is no knowledge of sickness they might incidentally make a call or a visit? It might seem severe when first inaugurated; but is not this the common-sense principle, the plain duty arising out of the relationship?

VISITING THE SICK.

Visiting the sick is a serious business, greatly overdone, to the injury of hundreds of bodies and souls. Ought any one to visit a sick person until called for? is a question really worth discussing. It is quite certain that all men ought not to visit all sick men, and that there ought to be some principle regulating this matter. It may be a kind of goodness of heart which leads a man to run in and see his acquaintances who are sick; but he may be the very man between whom and the sick person there are such physical and spiritual antagonisms that a visit from him would increase the sickness of the invalid.

But one thing seems to be well settled, that the initial motion is to be upon the part of the sick man. "Is any sick, let him call for the Elders." Let him determine whom he will have, and very naturally, as a Christian man, he will send for those who are the nearest akin to him spiritually.

OTHER DIRECTIONS FOR THE SICK.

In immediate connection follows what is written in the three following verses, 16, 17, 18:

"*Confess to one another your faults and pray for one another, that ye may be healed. Much availeth the inwrought supplication of a righteous man. Elijah was a man of like affections with us, and he prayed pressingly that it might not rain, and it rained not on the earth three years and six months. And again he prayed, and the heaven gave rain, and the earth brought forth her fruit.*"

This would seem to indicate that the prayer for healing was not to be offered until the patient had had an interview with those whom he had offended and confessed his fault. This is an important consideration generally overlooked. It is plain that no prayer would be of any avail for an unconfessing, unrepentant, uncharitable patient.

This must be read in strict connection with what went before. It is a direction to a sick man; one whose sickness has been brought on by his sin, or by some imprudence which preys upon his mind.

SICKNESS PRODUCED BY MENTAL TROUBLE.

Few persons who have never looked into it know what a large proportion of the sicknesses of the world come upon men because of some mental irregularity. Perhaps they are as many as are brought on by bodily excesses. Even when a man is temperate in eating and drinking, and manages his whole physical economy after the best known laws of hygiene, the troubles of his mind may make him sick. A business loss, an unrequited love, a fractured friendship, a disappointed hope, anxiety about wealth or reputation, about wife or child ; jealousy, envy, malice, hatred—any one of these may make a man sick. No one of delicate organization or good conscience can have a quarrel with a friend without depression of his bodily health. The remembrance of our faults toward others — faults which we are too proud to acknowledge, and which we defend in private to ourselves—will lower the tone of a man's health.

CONFESSION.

The case before us supposes a Christian who is sick, and who has committed no great crime, no crying sin, but a fault toward his brother. He is the man whose case was mentioned in the preceding verses. His faults had brought him to his bed, his sickness had brought him to penitence ; he desires to be forgiven and healed. He sends for the Church officials, who use first the physical agents of remedy and then engage in prayer. Now, says the Apostle, "Send for your brother, against whom you have committed a fault. Confess your fault to him ; perhaps that will bring him to perceiving that he has had faults towards you. When you have prayed together, you for him and he for you, and have come to be loving friends again, then all may go right, and the peace of your mind will advance the recovery of your body, and so you may be healed."

In this whole matter of confession it is important to guard against morbid feeling and mistaken action. Where another is concerned, and such a sin is committed that the acknowledgment to him or to the world would put him in no better position than he is now, why should there be any confession made? Confession to other than the offended party, or even to the injured party, may itself become injurious to a wide circle. The confession should not be made to a third party, but only to the party involved in the difficulty. Even a priest is bound to refuse to hear a "confession" which incriminates an absent party; as, for instance, where a man or woman confesses adultery, the confession may be taken in order that the person confessing may receive spiritual direction and help, but the partner in the sin must not be named, because he or she is not present and cannot be helped; and the pastor who would seek to make the penitent reveal the name of the co-sinner should be considered a scoundrel. It is my fault against my brother which I must confess *to my brother* alone. That confession must always be made in a truly devout spirit; in a spirit consistent with acts of prayer. It must not be done perfunctorily, merely to get through a duty, but must come from the heart, just as prayer must come from the heart; and must leave the confessor in that state of mind which prepares him to go to the Heavenly Father and invoke all blessings upon the brother whom he had offended.

And this points us to the ethical lesson on the other side, which is often overlooked. When my brother is convinced that he has committed a fault against me, and being sick and unable to visit me, sends for me and begins to make confession, I must not draw myself up haughtily and tell him I am glad he has come to his senses at length. I must not upbraid him for his fault. I must listen very patiently and humbly to his confession, examining my own heart to see whether there might not have been something in my conduct to betray my brother into his fault, and whether, also, I may not have so resented his fault as to be betrayed by indignation into a fault on my own part.

I must listen with the greatest gladness, seeing that he has been brought by the Spirit of God to such a state; and I must earnestly desire to be in as proper a moral position toward him. If all this be done, then, immediately after confession will follow forgiveness and prayer. He that had done the wrong and he that had received it will pray each for the other, and there will be real, unaffected love; and a state of love amongst all Christians is that which every man who loves our Lord Christ does most intensely long for.

LIMITATIONS.

It would seem that we must still read what is written as bearing upon the case of a sick man, whose sickness has been brought on by sin, and who sends for the Elders of his congregation to come and pray for his healing. All prayer is of avail, because prayer is the communion of the soul with God; and any man at any time may pray for a spiritual blessing. It is always right for any man to pray for such things as are distinctly promised in the Holy Scripture. Now the healing of every sick man is not so promised. The prayer for the healing of a sick man is a very special kind of prayer. It is not to be presented to Almighty God, unless the one who presents it, has wrought in him by the Holy Ghost, a conviction that in this case God intends to raise the man up. This seems a very important and much-overlooked matter. In a case of prayer-healing there are three factors necessary: (1) A righteous man to pray; (2) his offer of prayer; (3) that the prayer should be the product of some revelation from God, or powerful conviction in man's mind wrought by the Spirit of God, that He intends to heal the sick man.

ELIJAH'S PRAYERS.

It is plainly not God's intention to heal all the sick men or to feed all the hungry people by special or miraculous intervention. Widows and widows were in Israel in the days of Elijah, and yet he was sent only to a widow of Zarepta. There were sick people in multitudes in the time of the Apostles, and yet the Apostles were directed to heal only a few such, and in every case there seemed to be special antecedent direction as to which persons were to be restored to health. They "looked upon" the sick; it seemed to be a searching gaze in which there came to them the conviction that there was a case for which healing prayer might be made, failing which connection the prayer was not to be offered. All true prayer brings some spiritual blessing somewhere, but the prayers which are to affect the material world are "inwrought" prayers. All Elijah's prayers for Israel brought some blessings. But the cases cited by JAMES were cases of "inwrought" prayer, and because they so especially illustrated the profound meaning of our author, it may be well that we enter upon an examination of them.

While JAMES tells us that Elijah prayed "pressingly" that it might not rain, we learn from the Scriptures (1 Kings 17) that that prayer was founded upon a revelation from Jehovah, that He who is the Lord of Hosts, and who operates all the forces of nature incessantly, would withhold rain until Elijah should call for it, so that Elijah could go and stand before Ahab and say, "As

Jehovah, God of Israel, liveth, before whom I stand, there shall not be dew nor rain these years, but according to my word." If his conviction had not been founded on the word of God, his speech to the king would not only have been impertinent impudence but also outrageous blasphemy. He had determined that his word should be according to the word of Jehovah. So, after the lapse of years, we have that thrilling description of Elijah, with the priests of Baal assembled on Carmel, settling allegiance by the test of the God who should answer prayer. It was *after* the decision of that question that Elijah went up to the top of Carmel, and cast himself down upon the earth, and put his face between his knees; but it was *before* that decision that the word of the Lord had come to Elijah, saying, " Go show thyself unto Ahab, and I shall send rain upon the earth."

In both cases, the case of the drought and the case of the rain, there was in Elijah an "inwrought" prayer, inwrought by the Spirit and the word of the Lord. The energy in this case was in the word of the Lord that came to the man before he prayed, not in the prayer, although it was a "pressing" prayer, and the prayer was not less pressing because it was made upon the promise; on the contrary, the very foundation which the promise afforded imparted increased energy to the prayer. A man who in our day should undertake to shut off rain for three years and then set open the fountains of the clouds would be a mere fanatic. So would be any man who went about to pray for the absolute and immediate healing of every sick man without a warrant from God. Does the Lord now ever give such a conviction? There are cases so well attested that we must believe He sometimes does. Notwithstanding the irregularities, the fanaticisms, the fooleries, and the frauds attendant upon so much of the so-called faith cures, we must not allow ourselves to be carried away from a common-sense view of the truths revealed in the Sacred Scripture.

INWROUGHT PRAYER.

God hath ordained prayer. It must therefore be His intention that prayer shall be profitable. He has directed the modes of prayer which will be acceptable to Him. He has indicated the fields of prayer in which it may be cultivated. He has afforded specific promises. On those promises we may confidently come to Him in prayer. The history of exceptional cases in which the Spirit of God seems to have made a powerful impression on the spirits of intelligent, unfanatic, devout, and obedient Christian souls, and the answers by which such "inwrought" prayers have been followed, do all confirm the faith of simple-hearted people. We are to pray for one another, and always pray in most humble submission to the will of God. When the prayers are made for other than such spiritual things as are covenanted in the explicit promises of Holy Scripture, we may not go around praying for every sick man, whether he be penitent or impenitent, faithful or reprobate, nor pray in such a manner as would indicate that we are seeking to have our wills overrule the will of Almighty God.

A case like this can readily be supposed. A man devoutly engaged in the service of God is sick. He has peace with God. He could die in the odor of sanctity and the triumphs of faith. If I had command of all the forces in the universe I might bring that man up from his sickness into high health, and he might go into such courses as would be fatal to him and destructive to society. *That* I might not be able to foresee; but God knows all things. It may be utterly impracticable to answer both prayers, the prayer for the restoration of his health and the prayer for the salvation of his soul. Restoration to health would be ruin, the salvation of his soul means death.

As prayer is set forth in the Sacred Scripture, there is nothing in it to contravene either science or common sense. There are few ways in which Christians can advance their religion more than by dealing with Holy Scripture in the light of plain reason; reason that is sanctified by humble submission to the will of God.

THE LAST SENTENCE.

We come now to the last sentence in this remarkable letter:

"*Brethren, if any among you wander from the truth and any turn him back, let him know that he who turneth back a sinner from the wandering of his way shall save a soul from death and shall cover a multitude of sins.*"

While logically intimate with what just precedes it, this saying of the Apostle closes the circle of his instructions, and sets before us the loftiest employment, and the greatest enjoyment, and the noblest glory that can come to humanity. The logical connection seems to be this, that where there has been mutual confession after disagreements that were injurious to soul and body and prayer had been made for each other, the result would be the saving of a soul from death.

TRUTH.

Truth is the purest thing in the universe. Truth is the most powerful thing in the universe. Truth is the most enduring thing in the universe. Truth makes God to be God, and when God came in the flesh, the brightest crown He could place upon His own head, the noblest name He could give to His personality was "*The Truth.*" The greatest work in which God can be engaged is the propagation of the truth. Truth to be truth, must be absolutely unmixed. There can be nothing ugly, nothing foul, nothing debasing in it. It is the very cleanliness of cleanliness. It is flawless and spotless. It is this which gives it such force; it is this which makes it so enduring; it is this which makes it so dear to the holy heart of God. It is this into which He pours the molten contents of His own divine heart. More than if He had said, "I am King of kings and Lord of lords and the Judge of all men" was the word which Jesus the Christ spake when He said of Himself, "I AM THE TRUTH." There was nothing to which God could be a martyr but the truth, and Jesus said (John 18 : 37), "For this cause came I into the world, that I should bear witness to the truth," that is, be "a martyr to the truth." And when He went away He prophesied that His place would be taken by the "Spirit of Truth," thus giving this name to the Holy Ghost (John 16 : 13).

WHAT ERROR IS.

It is to be noted that all the wrongs in the universe begin by a wandering from the truth. There never could be sin which is not preceded by some divergence from the truth. This is so in every department of human thought, emotion and action. The word "error" means "wandering"; and so JAMES speaks of *sin* as *wandering from the truth*. It is because the sin begins in some slight departure, in the man, from that which is true, leading to a departure of the affections, which produces a departure in the outward life, that men should be strenuously anxious to know the truth, especially the truth as to their highest things, **their highest connections**; the truth **as** to God, the truth as to their own nature, the truth as to their relations to God, the truth as to their own character.

When men talk of the valuelessness of doctrine, and say it does not matter what a man believes so that his life is right, they show their absolute ignorance of the whole subject. It is as if one should say, it is no matter what disease a man has so long as he has health. The outward life of a man is the product of his character, and his character is the product of his creed. If there be one rule without an exception this must be the rule. It certainly is the counterpart in the spiritual world of the fact in physics that no stream ever rises above its source. Now, the source of the outer life is the creed. Nay, it is something still stronger than that. A man is just what he believes, no more, no less. Neither God nor the devil can make him any more or any less. To make any change in him the good or the bad need not strive to mould his outer life, or by any other process attempt to change his character except by efforts to make a change in his creed. If he have believed error, to make him a good man he must be brought to faith in the truth; if he have such faith, to make him a bad man all that is necessary is to break the hold of his faith on the truth.

WHAT CREED IS.

"As a man thinks in his heart, so is he." Now the phrase, " thinks in his heart," is equivalent to "creed," creed being compounded of two words, signifying that form of belief to which I give my heart. If any one shall object to this that there are so many who profess a good creed and lead a bad life, the reply is ready. In such a case the creed is only professed, it is not held. Indeed, a creed is not that which a man holds at all; it is that which holds him. When a man once comes into vital connection with the creed, he is never its master; it is always his.

The objection to doctrinal preaching has just this weak foundation. There is no preaching so primarily important as doctrinal preaching. There is no knowledge of the Bible so important as a knowledge of its doctrines. These are what shape a man's character, not the poetry, the beauty, the sublimity of the Bible. Let every man be sure that his principles are more important than his behavior, or than any formulated rules of life he may make. Indeed these rules will be the product of principles if they have any power. A man who had any principles might have all the rules of ethics committed to memory, and capable of being summoned at any moment, and yet they would be powerful only as founded upon principles. If the man have good rules and a bad memory, his rules may be forgotten; but if he have the principles he can on any emergency construct the rule. This seems to be as true in the moral life as it is in mathematics. If a mathematical principle be made perfectly familiar to the mind of the child, he may forget the formal rule in his arithmetic, but this principle which he knows will enable him to reconstruct the rule whenever needed.

A GRAND POSSIBILITY.

Then JAMES points to a grand possibility. It is possible for one human being to turn another back from his intellectual and moral and spiritual wanderings; and this grand possibility ought to make all good men very earnest in their anxiety to learn how this is to be done. Plainly, it cannot be done by force; plainly, it cannot be done by compressing a man's outward behavior by rules. All persecution is impertinent; it is out of place in a case like this. There is but one way in which this work can be begun properly. As the trouble was in a man's wandering from the truth, the first point to be gained is somehow to make a fresh connection of that man's soul with the truth. He is as a planet that hath broken away from the power of attraction and gone wildly off at a destructive tangent. Nothing can be done for a universe going to chaos until a mode be found by which there shall be a restoration of the proper play of attractive forces. To save a man, therefore, he must be brought under the power of some saving truth. It must get the dominance of him, and rule him to that degree that he will no longer wander away.

When He who called Himself "The Truth" was offering to His Father that sublime prayer with which he closed His career just before His betrayal, He prayed for those dear disciples that they might be sanctified through "Thy Truth." It is a blessed thing when such a saving truth can be brought to bear upon a wandering soul, and thrice blessed is the man who brings that truth to bear upon his fellow-man by its embodiment in his own rounded, beautiful, truth-ruled life.

A WHOLESOME REACTION.

Every Christian man should engage all his powers in the work of striving to save his own soul and the souls of his fellow-men; not by any charm, or magical process, but by striving as far as possible, to bring wandering souls under the power of saving truths. One great stimulus to this work is the reflection that nothing is so saving, so purifying, so elevating to any man's own soul, as the work of striving to save the souls of other men. We waste our time in dreaming of heaven and wishing for heaven. The best preparation for the world to come is the proper employment of all our powers in achieving the greatest things possible to us in this world. If the brethren of JAMES had been spending all their time in bringing themselves and others under the power of sanctifying truth, they would not have needed a single admonition contained in this pungent **epistle.** If the whole Christian Church were engaged in this work there would be no space nor time for bickering, quarrelling, persecution, schism, and all the other wrongs which have stained the history of the Church.

THE GRANDEST HUMAN WORK.

Each Christian man is stimulated to this work, because it is the grandest possible to any human being. To know the truth is the highest function and capability of the intellect. To bring the truth to bear upon other minds, is the loftiest and noblest exercise of man's moral powers. What else is equal to the achievement of saving a soul? Is the writing of a poem? Is the carving of a statue? Is the painting of a picture? Is the erection of a monument? Is the creation of a reputation? All these things will perish. When Napoleon was told by the painter that the canvas would carry his portrait down five centuries, he exclaimed, "Is this all?" His mind was comprehensive enough to see that, in comparison with the æons, cycles and eternities of the future, five hundred years were an insignificant portion of time.

SOUL-DEATH.

The Holy Scriptures speak of the *death of the soul;* "the soul that sinneth, it shall die." That fact, which never could have been ascertained without a direct revelation from Him who knows eternity, is imparted to us without any definite explanations of the modes and meanings of this death. We learn from nature that a body may die. We learn from revelation that a soul may die. We learn from nature that a sick body may be recovered. We learn from revelation that a sick soul may be healed. As there are physical remedies for bodily diseases, there is a spiritual remedy for soul maladies. That remedy is *the truth*. Only as a man is sanctified in the truth can he come into soul health; and, if he remain in soul sickness, he must eventually die a soul death, whatever that is. What that terrible catastrophe is, who can comprehend? The Scriptures tells us *the fact*, and leave us with a dim intimation of all its dreadful accessories. Now, to bring a soul back from its wanderings to the truth, that is to Christ, is to secure for that soul eternal life, which "is a gift of God through Jesus Christ our Lord." Out of material things it is impossible to construct an enduring monument; but he that hath saved a soul from death has secured one thing permanent through eternity. There can not be any other work so grand as this. There cannot be any other work that myriads of years from this time shall give such profound satisfaction as to save a soul from death.

COVERING SIN.

Error and truth are polar extremes, like life and death. The one thing that irradiates the universe is truth; the one thing which is a dark spot upon the universe is sin. It is the one thing which God abhors; He cannot tolerate it. "Now," says JAMES, "when one converts a sinner from the error of his ways, he not only saves a soul from death, but he hides a multitude of sins." This word "cover," or "hide," is a biblical phrase, first in the Old Testament and then in the New, to signify forgiveness, as when (Ps. 32: 1) it is written, "Blessed is he whose transgression is forgiven, whose sin is covered." This Hebrew parallelism shows us that "covering" means "forgiving" when it is the act of God. "He that hideth his own sin shall not prosper," but he whose sin God puts out of sight and out of remembrance, is a happy man. And so any sinner may pray, "Hide Thy face from my sins and blot out all mine iniquities." It is a truth old as the Book of Proverbs, "that love covereth all sins" (10: 12); a truth which is repeated by an Apostle, "Charity shall cover a multitude of sins" (1 Peter 4: 8). To the man whose whole nature is turned about, who, instead of *wandering*, that is to say, leading a lawless life, is brought under the guiding and sustaining power of a saving truth, the sins of the past are forgiven, many or few, light or grave, for there comes to him the complete forgiveness of the Divine Father.

There is something more stimulating than that. If I let my neighbor go on in sin I must remind myself of the reduplicating power of sinfulness; how it grows, how "one sinner destroys much good," how one sinner makes many sinners, some of whom are tenfold worse than himself. Let any one consider for a moment what might have been the increased badness of the world if Paul, or Augustine, or John Newton, or any other sinner who has been "plucked as the brand out of the burning" had not been converted when he was converted, but had gone on to an old age increasing the number and influence of his own sins, and multiplying corrupting agencies in the community. What is not seen cannot be well calculated. If the conversion had not taken place the injuriousness of each man's life would have been very manifest to the world. What he was saved from doing by his conversion can never be known; but a sober calculation of the probabilities can be made from what is known of the life when it was bad.

TRUE LIBERTY.

If a man shall convert his neighbor from the error of his ways the good that neighbor shall do after his conversion will become known to the world in some measure. But all the sins he would have committed but for the conversion would be covered up and hidden away from human eyes. With these two things before us, namely, the prevention of a life of sinfulness, a thing so offensive to our Heavenly Father, and the production of a life radiant in truth, which is so delightful to our

Heavenly Father, the one great work ought to be (to every moral man, to every man capable of ethical ideas, to every man who applies his common sense to the problems of human life and human destiny) the turning away of men from their wanderings, and fixing them in the realm, under the reign, of moral law. There, and there only, is liberty; liberty for which millions of souls have sighed; liberty for which millions of men have died. Liberty, in whose name, as the dying Mme. Roland said, so many crimes had been committed, real, manly, moral, intellectual, spiritual liberty, is secured only to the man who has been converted from the error of his ways by a conversion from the error of his thoughts. Even as JAMES'S great brother said, " Ye shall know the truth and the truth shall make you free."

To secure personal and civil liberty what have not men endured of hunger, and thirst, and shipwreck, and imprisonment, and betrayal, and scourging, and torture, and death? With the increase of the ages grows the glowing fame of men who have "made way for liberty," even when those men have been fighting and dying for only personal and civil liberty, themselves often the most abject slaves of tyrannical sinfulness, like Danton and Robespierre and other wretched leaders of French revolution, and more modern agitators of society, who have yet to learn the first letters in the alphabet of freedom, till they shall rise to know that law is as essentially the basis of liberty as life is the basis of feeling.

IMMORTAL FAME.

Can any human being do too much to secure the lives, the liberties, the fortunes of human souls? To such men not any monuments are erected upon earth, but there is immortal fame for them in eternity, because they wrought to secure souls from death and keep those souls in liberty. Does any one wonder that a man with such great intellect as the Apostle Paul turned aside from every path of human ambition to walk this way of usefulness, although it led him through all kinds of difficulties down to martyrdom? The wonder is that in every age there are not more to imitate that member of the early Christian Church who sold himself as a slave to a heathen family that he might gain access to it. That family, in reward of faithful labor amongst them and their conversion to the truth, set him free. He used his freedom only for the purpose of saving souls from death and hiding a multitude of sins, and so, sold himself again a slave to the Governor of Sparta, with like success and fresh trophies to the cause of truth. Let that man consider himself very small, whatever be the amount of his brains and his financial fortune, whatever be the sphere of his operations, whatever be the measure of his earthly success, whose life is not laid out in any sphere of science, politics, merchandise, or social life, to the great work of turning himself and his fellow-men away from their errors back to the truth.

We can scarcely conceive the permanency of our identity without the continuance of our memory. If a man in passing into another sphere, could drink, at the gate of the new department, some nepenthe which should make him forget all that is past, while he would appear to some external eye to be the same person, he himself would have no consciousness of identity with the man who had crossed that portal. If a man is to exist millions of years after his death, if one can speak of years in considering the admeasurements of eternity, to be himself he must be able to remember himself. Let a man now think what will probably be the precious things of memory a myriad of years hence, when all the present state of terrestrial affairs shall have passed away, all its history destroyed, all its monuments forgotten. Will it be the accumulation of a few poor, pitiful millions of dollars, most of which he could not use even while in the flesh? Will it be that his name was in the newspapers of his day? Will it be that he had a momentary thrill of physical enjoyment? What will it be? If, amid all these things, he was ever able to turn one soul from the error of his way, and stopped and dried up a stream of sin, and brought that soul into the possession of eternal life, will not the memory of *that* in the world to come be to the man something in value outweighing all thrones and crowns and sceptres and terrestrial palaces?

With the suggestion of such a sublime possibility, our author concludes his epistle. He lifts us from the low conception of ethics as being something which furnishes rules for the regulation of a little life, and places us and sets it in the light of its true relation with the things which are unseen and eternal.

"Sunshine for Dark Hours,"

By CHARLES F. DEEMS, D.D., LL.D.,

Author of "Weights and Wings," "Home Altar," etc., and Editor of "Christian Thought."

A book for invalids. The matter of this book is drawn from a wide range of reading, observation and experience, and is a genuine aid to contentment, comfort and relief.

The tone of the book is indicative of strength gained by submission, an entire and hearty acquiescence in the will of God. It will brighten dark hours. If you have sick friends brighten their rooms and hearts by sending a copy of this good and helpful book. It is printed in large type and clear page, and is particularly adapted to the invalid.

Price, 25 Cents, By Mail, 30 Cents.

WILBUR B. KETCHAM, Publisher,
13 Cooper Union, New York.

SERMONS

—BY—

CHARLES F. DEEMS, D.D., LL. D.,

Pastor of the Church of the Strangers, Author of "Weights and Wings," "Home Altar," etc., and Editor of "Christian Thought."

PARTIAL LIST OF SERMONS.

Christianity Confronting Frivolous Skepticism. Are Christians Narrow? A Despicable Minister. No Room for Jesus. Trinity of Excellence. What Jesus saw from the Cross. Christ's Cure for Trouble. Christ's Pledge. The Memorial Supper. Characteristics of a Sinful Life. Secret Discipleship. Reconciliation. Influence of Christianity on Life.

The Baltimore Episcopal Methodist says:—We welcome them with much pleasure, and commend them to our readers and the Christian public generally. They are sound in doctrine, chaste and beautiful in style, thoroughly evangelical, and eminently practical.

---

8 vo., Cloth. 304 pages. Price, $1.50.

WILBUR B. KETCHAM, Publisher,

13 Cooper Union, New York.

THE GOSPEL IN NATURE

By H. C. McCOOK, D.D.,
Vice-President Academy of Natural Sciences, Philadelphia, Author of "Agricultural Ant of Texas," "Tenants of an Old Farm," and "The Honey and Occident Ants."

A series of popular discourses on Scripture truths derived from facts in nature.

N. Y. Observer says:—They are written somewhat in the vein of Professor Drummond's "Natural Law in the Spiritual World," and will be welcomed by intelligent readers who are awake to the discussion which is going on in the world over the Book of Books and the Book of Nature.

Interior.—The author ranges through earth and air, finding exemplifications of the wisdom and power of the Almighty Creator in the hail and snow, the rain and the rainbow, flowers and vines, and showing both forcibly and beautifully, how the elements of nature can be used to illustrate and work out the Divine Will, and the knowledge of that will toward man.

JOHN HALL, D.D., *Pastor of the Fifth Avenue Presbyterian Church, New York.*— "It takes familiar facts from the works of God and employs them, with learning and devoutness, for the illustration of vital truths, only learned from the word of God. Dr. McCook has here, as elsewhere, used his talent for natural history wisely and effectively; and his work is practical and adapted to our times.

12 mo., Cloth, 380 pp. Price $1.25 net.

WILBUR B. KETCHAM, Publisher,
13 Cooper Union, New York.

FAIRY TALES
—OF—
SCIENCE,
BEING
POPULAR SCIENTIFIC PAPERS,
BY
Rev. J. GORDON McPHERSON,

Author of "Strathmore: Past and Present," "Superstition and Scepticism," Etc.

The author has "the way of putting" the technical language of specialists so as to present the result of their inquiries in forms likely to convey instruction to the general reader. To men who lived fifty years ago an account of these wonderful discoveries would have read like so many "fairy tales," hence the title. The index is particularly full, in order that reference to details may be most convenient. It will prove a helpful book to all, particularly to the clergy as a book from which many illustrations can be culled.

Among the many subjects are the following: "Formation of Dew," "Color of Water," "Dust and Fogs," "Sun Spots," "The Universal Day," "Counting of Dust-Particles in Air," "Bright Clouds on a Dark Night-Sky," "Water Pipes and Frost," etc., etc.,

---

12 mo., Cloth, 277 Pages.   Price, $1.25.

WILBUR B. KETCHAM, Publisher,
13 Cooper Union, New York.

OUR REST DAY,

ITS ORIGIN, HISTORY, AND CLAIMS, WITH SPECIAL REFERENCE TO PRESENT DAY NEEDS.

—BY—

THOMAS HAMILTON, D. D.

The *New York Christian Advocate* says: In the book we find the entire subject of "Sabbath observance" most thoroughly and candidly considered. All the popular arguments for relaxation of the plain Bible command are met and treated at length. The chapters are headed, "How Old Art Thou?" "Traces of the Sabbath in Ancient Lands and Literature," "A Curious Theory," "The Sabbath not a Jewish Institution," The Decalogue and the Sabbath," "Christ and the Sabbath," "The Apostles and the Sabbath," "The Change of Day," The Church of Rome and the Sabbath," and then the author turns to the various methods of trade and amusement to infringe upon the "Rest Day." Two chapters have been added upon "How the Conflict Goes On," and "The Conclusion of the Whole Matter." Any one who wishes information upon this subject, now one of the foremost in popular interest, will find this little book of practical value.

Rev. C. H. Spurgeon says: "Other works have been good, but none could have been better. It is as interesting as it is instructive, and we give it our hearty praise."

12 mo. Cloth, 185 pp., Price, 75 Cents.

WILBUR B. KETCHAM, Publisher,

13 Cooper Union, New York.

THE KING'S SON

OR,

A MEMOIR OF BILLY BRAY,

By F. W. BOURNE.

The New York Christian Advocate says:—"Of Billy Bray, the famous Methodist preacher of Cornwall, Eng., it may be truly said "he yet speaketh," although he has been dead more than twenty years. It is reported that at least six hundred persons are known to have been led to CHRIST by reading his biography. These converts are found in all parts of the world, and come from almost every position in life. Noted infidels, eminent formalists, and cultivated scholars, as well as obscure and unlearned men, have been drawn into the Kingdom of grace by this fascinating story. The most noted preacher of the age frequently finds the striking illustrations which enrich his sermons in the Life of Billy Bray."

TWENTY-SEVENTH EDITION NOW READY.

18 mo., Cloth.   119 pp.   Price, 50 Cents.

WILBUR B. KETCHAM, Publisher,
13 Cooper Union, New York.

www.ingramcontent.com/pod-product-compliance
Lightning Source LLC
Chambersburg PA
CBHW030010240426
43672CB00007B/891